HOLIDAY WALKS
in
IRELAND:
CONNACHT

Paddy Dillon

Copyright © 2001, Paddy Dillon

Published by Sigma Leisure – an imprint of Sigma Press, 1 South Oak Lane, Wilmslow, Cheshire SK9 6AR, England.

British Library Cataloguing in Publication Data
A CIP record for this book is available from the British Library.

ISBN: 1-85058-754-X

Typesetting and Design by: Sigma Press, Wilmslow, Cheshire.

Cover design by: The Agency, Macclesfield, Cheshire

Printed by: MFP Design & Print

Cover Photograph: main picture – Benbulbin; smaller pictures, from left – Mámean; Ben Lugmore; Castlegal Range.

Photographs: the author

Maps: Michael Gilbert

Contents

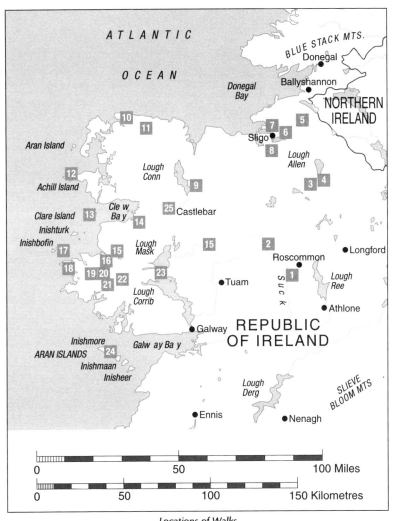

Locations of Walks

KEY TO MAPS

- - - > - - -   Route and direction

───────────   Main road

───────────   Minor road

++++++++++++++   Railway

Louge   River or Stream

□ Building   † Church

Built-up area ○ Megalithic Tomb

▲ Signal Tower △ Hight marker

▲ Trees   P Parking

PO Post Office ④ Route Notes

Introduction

Connacht is one of the four ancient Provinces of Ireland, consisting of the counties of Galway, Mayo, Sligo, Leitrim and Roscommon. It is bounded on almost three sides by the sea, with Donegal Bay to the north, the Atlantic Ocean wrapped around the west, and Galway Bay to the South. Inland, the mighty River Shannon marks the eastern boundary of Connacht. The Province is almost an island within the larger island of Ireland.

Walking opportunities around Connacht are rich and varied. The coastline is heavily indented, so that there are many fine, rugged headlands and cliffs, including the tallest sea cliffs in Ireland. The coast breaks up into dozens of islands, including Achill Island, which is the largest island off the Irish coast. Other popular islands include the Aran Islands, Inishbofin and Clare Island. The coast also features Ireland's only true fjord; the long and narrow inlet of Killary Harbour.

Moving inland, there are ranges of rugged mountains, including the Twelve Bens of Connemara, Maum Turk Mountains, the Nephin Beg Range and the Ox Mountains. Most of the mountains are made of hard quartzite, but there are also mountains made of limestone and sandstone layers around Sligo and North Leitrim, and in the Arigna Mountains in North Roscommon. The highest mountain in the Province of Connacht is Mweelrea, rising proudly above the sea at Killary Harbour. There are mountains that stand in splendid isolation, such as Knocknarea, Nephin and Croagh Patrick, also known as 'The Reek'. It is fair to say that Croagh Patrick is Ireland's most often climbed mountain, with an estimated 100,000 people a year reaching its summit. It is Ireland's Holy Mountain and has been revered as such from Druidical times, through Christian times, to the present day.

As walking has increased in popularity, a series of waymarked walking trails have appeared through the countryside. These are generally low-level, but often brush shoulders with the higher mountains. The Western Way was the first to be blazed around Connacht, and the Bangor Trail, Foxford Way and Sligo Way were linked into its course. Another series of trails that link together include the Leitrim Way, Miner's Way and Historical Trail. A very interesting low-level route, taking in fields and riversides, is the Suck Valley Way. The latest trail to be waymarked is the Connemara Way, offering a fine loop even further west than the Western Way. The waymarked trails are remarkably under-used, when compared to some of the popular mountains in Connacht, or the growing number of walking festivals.

Mythology and history are closely intertwined with the landscape throughout Ireland, and Connacht is no exception. As you wander around the countryside you'll be reminded constantly of thousands of years of human settlement. There are Neolithic tombs and Bronze Age ritual sites, as well as early Christian churches and Anglo Norman castles and abbeys. Add to this the 'Big Houses' of the gentry and the humble cottages of the farmers and fishermen, and you'll see history piled on top of history wherever you go.

For some reason, the Province of Connacht has often been settled by waves of dispossessed people from other parts of Ireland. The mythical race known as the Firbolgs were allotted the Province after being defeated by the divine Tuatha De Danann, who themselves occupied the rest of Ireland. In later historical times, the O'Flahertys settled in the area after being dispossessed by waves of Anglo-Norman settlers. The local people used to pray for deliverance from the 'fury of the O'Flahertys'. After the Cromwellian campaigns, which were particularly brutal in Ireland, large areas of the country were planted and the defeated population were told they could go to 'Hell or Connacht'.

The writer T. H. White, in 'The Godstone and the Blackymor' observed the following: *'Ireland is a melting pot of conquered cultures, stone men and bronze men and iron men, of Celts and Vikings and Anglo-Normans, driven remorselessly westwards by a volcano of European history, pressed finally together against the rim of the Atlantic in their promontory forts, between the devil of the new weapon and the deep sea. Their Gods go with them. Duk Duk dancers and Druids, Fir Bolg and Tuatha De Danann, Baal and Beltaine, Crom Cruach and Cromwell, the conquered conquerors, enslaved, revengeful, charged with ancient powers.'*

Irish history at a glance and Connacht in particular

7,000 BC – Mesolithic hunter-gatherers arrive in Ireland. Their presence is indicated only by small finds of discarded flint tools, and hardly any evidence of their presence is found in Connacht.

4,000 BC – Neolithic farmers slash and burn forests, enclose fields, till the land and keep livestock. They buried their dead in court tombs, passage tombs and portal tombs, often made of immense blocks of stones, usually with cairns heaped on top of them. There are numerous remains of these types around Connacht, notably Moytura, the Bricklieve Mountains and Knocknarea. Their field systems can be most easily studied at the Ceide Fields near Ballycastle.

2,000 BC – Early Bronze Age people used metal tools and created a distinctive pottery that has earned them the name Beaker People. They built wedge tombs and stone circles, as well as erecting prominent standing stones. In Connacht these structures can be identified all the way from Moytura to Connemara.

1,200 BC – Late Bronze Age times are characterised by a sudden increase in the amount of metalwork produced, suggesting some quite well organised industry, but also indicating a fair amount of strife across the country.

200 BC – The Iron Age in Ireland is generally taken to coincide with the arrival of the first Celts and their distinctive culture. Weapons of bronze and iron are common, and decorative features incorporate distinctive spiral designs. Hill forts were constructed; as well as smaller 'raths' or 'ring forts'. Some of them are so complex that they are thought to have been 'royal' enclosures. A rich folklore has been passed on through the oral tradition concerning tales of bravery, honour and magic. One of the most colourful characters in Irish mythology is Queen Maeve of Connacht.

400 AD – The early Christian period in Ireland was slow to start, but from the year 432, when St. Patrick started his mission, interest in the new religion developed apace. St. Patrick's main achievement in Connacht was his forty-day and forty-night fast on the summit of Croagh Patrick, which he reached by following a Druidical causeway across country. Other Christian leaders and hermits established small churches and retreats, often in wild and remote places. People continued to construct 'raths', but as Christian settlements grew, some more substantial stone structures were built.

795 AD – The Viking colonisation of the Irish coast commences and settlements are established. Irish monasteries build round towers for defence, but suffer a series of raids. Viking warrior burials and house sites are known in Connacht.

1014 – The Battle of Clontarf, in which the Irish, led by Brian Boru, achieved a resounding victory over the Vikings. Although defeated, many Vikings remained in Ireland.

1150 – Large religious orders from Europe were already building big abbeys in Ireland before the arrival of the Anglo-Normans in 1170. Medieval Ireland saw the abandonment of the smaller Irish rural monasteries, and the foundation of larger monasteries, as well as 'motte and baileys' and large stone castles. There are sporadic attempts to settle English colonists in Ireland, and sporadic uprisings by the Irish. Many colonists intermarry with the Irish, becoming 'more Irish than the Irish themselves'.

1594 – The start of the Nine Years War, with the O'Neills leading the Irish against English. The 'Battle of the Curlews' in 1599 in Connacht was a victory for the Irish, but it was followed in 1607 by the 'Flight of the Earls' leaving the Irish virtually leaderless.

1649 – Cromwell commences a brutal campaign in Ireland, completed in 1653 when the Connacht island of Inishbofin finally falls. English settlers occupy confiscated Irish estates. The dispossessed are told to go to 'Hell or Connacht'.

1690 – William of Orange sweeps through Ireland, finally defeating King James at the Battle of the Boyne. The campaign was followed by the imposition of the harsh, anti-Catholic Penal Laws.

1798 – The Irish rebel against English rule, aided by the French. The French landed and swept through Connacht, totally routing the English at Castlebar. John Moore became President of the provisional Republic of Connacht for one week. The rebellion was crushed, followed by the Act of Union in 1800.

1845 – The Great Famine, caused by the failure of the potato crop year after year. Ireland's population was around 8 million, but around 2 million died or emigrated in those few years. Connacht was especially hard-hit and there are still many deserted village sites to be seen around the Province.

1879 – The formation of the Land League to campaign for fair rents results in the 'Land War' in which tenants are pitted against landlords. Michael Davitt of Connacht formulated the principles of the Land League and attracted great followings in pursuit of the cause.

1903 – The British naval fleet anchors in Killary Harbour as King Edward VIII and Queen Alexanda make a royal tour of Connemara.

1916 – The Easter Rising, followed in 1921 by the Anglo Irish Treaty, followed by the Civil War throughout the 1920s as the Irish Free State was formed. Even in remote parts of Connacht there were shootings and troubles. By 1948 the Free State became the Republic of Ireland.

1990 – Mary Robinson, a native of Connacht, was the first woman to be elected President of Ireland.

Practicalities

Maps

The Ordnance Survey of Ireland publishes 1:50,000 Discovery maps that cover the whole Province of Connacht. There is also an Ordnance Survey 1:25,000 map of the Aran Islands. Independent mapmaker Harveys publish a 1:30,000 Superwalker Map of Connemara. These maps often show the extent of the waymarked trails and give other clues about access along roads, bog roads and forest tracks. Accurate contouring is a great help in the upland regions. Ordnance Survey maps are available through good bookshops and the bigger newsagents. It is also possible to order them through the Ordnance Survey in Britain, or from specialist map suppliers and bookshops.

Weather

The Province of Connacht is generally wide open to whatever weather is coming in from the Atlantic Ocean. While rainfall is common, it is by no means continuous, and in between showers the air can be crystal clear, so that the colours of the landscape are vibrant. Cool, moist air from the Atlantic is forced over mountain ranges, resulting in the formation of clouds and rainfall. In some cases the mountains will be covered in mist, so that you should always carry a map and compass and have the ability to use them. Waterproofs are essential, though if you're completing low-level walks with a good forecast, you might leave them behind. There are no real extremes of weather. Heatwaves in summer and snowfalls in winter tend to be short-lived. The amount of rainfall and poor drainage has resulted in the formation of extensive blanket bogs on the mountains and often in the valleys too. The compacted dead vegetation, known as peat or 'turf' is cut and dried for fuel in the summer to last out the winter.

Walking and access

The Province of Connacht has a system of waymarked trails that are remarkably underused, as well as informal mountain walks that can be quite busy. There are also walking festivals you can attend, and the most spectacular one is undoubtedly the Castlebar International Four-Day Walks. The access situation isn't easy to understand. The waymarked trails have been negotiated by 'wayleaves' and can be closed at any time for any reason. They are not to be regarded as rights of way. Even when routes are locally regarded as a right of way, there is very little legal protection for them, and the general concensus is that the landowner can do what he likes with his property. There is generally no great objection to walkers taking to the hills and mountains, or following bog roads, and virtually all state forests are open to the public. It is not a good idea to take dogs into the countryside, and you should always respect the land across which you walk. Since the passing of the 1995 Occupiers Liability Act, which everyone thought would lead to greater access around Ireland, a number of brightly coloured notices forbidding access have appeared. At the time of writing, no access problems are known on any of the routes in this guidebook.

Public transport

The majority of walks in this guidebook were researched using public transport. The main operator in the Province of Connacht is Bus Éireann, though a few walks can be accessed using the Iarnród Éireann rail network. There are other small operators, such as Michael Nee's buses in Connemara, and if you're travelling to the islands then you'll need to check ferry services too. Bear in mind that public transport in such a remote part of Ireland can be pretty infrequent, but if you check timetables carefully you'll realise that there is always a way of getting to a place, tying in with accommodation, completing a walk and getting away again. Bus Éireann services can be checked on 01-8366111, and comprehensive annual timetables for all services are published in book form.

Accommodation

You'll be spoilt for choice in the Province of Connacht. You can stay anywhere from splendid castles to humble hostels. You'll find a fine selection of hotels, guesthouses, farmhouses and bed and breakfasts in between. Whether you choose to stay in the major towns or out in the countryside, there is generally a good range of accommodation. If you want a full meals service or any other extra facility, then check in advance. Comprehensive accommodation listings are available from the Irish Tourist Board, either from their head office in Dublin, or from any office in Ireland and even overseas. If you use the tourist board's listings, then the accommodation you choose will be 'approved', which means it will have been inspected and will conform to standards applied by the tourist board.

Language

The Province of Connacht is one of the strongholds of the Irish language. There are places in the extreme west where Irish is the everyday language of local people, though English is always understood. It can be quite an experience staying in the 'Gaeltacht' areas when summer language schools are in full swing. Even a very basic grasp of the language helps enormously when interpreting placenames in the countryside, which are often very descriptive, or point to some remote historical event or feature in the landscape.

Walk 1:
Athleague, Castlecoote & Castlestrange
A riverside ramble

This gentle walk from Athleague makes use of field paths and quiet country roads. The stretch through Castlecoote and Castlestrange is along the Suck Valley Way, running close to the River Suck. It is unusual to find low-level access to so many fields in Ireland, but along the course of the Suck Valley Way it has been achieved with the wholehearted co-operation of farmers and the provision of all the necessary stiles and footbridges. Despite the low-level nature of the terrain, and the acres of good pasture, there are also areas of marsh and wild woodlands that you can spot.

Grade: Easy

Distance: 18km (11 miles)

Time: 6½ hours (including an hour for lunch)

Start & Finish: On the bridge at Athleague 827577

Map: Ordnance Survey of Ireland Discovery 40

How to get there

> *By car:* Athleague is on the N63 road between Galway and Longford, but it could just as easily be approached by anyone using the N60 between Athlone and Castlebar. In this case, you would approach the village as signposted from Roscommon Town. Despite being a small place, Athleague is notable for the 'Kepak' meat processing plant, which is very well known throughout the West of Ireland.
>
> *By bus:* Bus Éireann table number 425 links Athleague with Galway and Longford. Table number 457 is a Wednesday only link with Roscommon and Ballina.

Necessities: Boots as the low-lying fields can be wet; **waterproofs** if rain is forecast; **money** for food and drink at Castlecoote and Athleague; **check the state of the river** as parts may be impassable during winter flooding.

Notes: The Suck Valley Way forms the basis for this circuit, but there is also a lengthy link on minor roads between the route at Rookwood and Castlecoote. The circuit is more or less defined by the course of the waymarked route and the availability of bridges over the river. There are bridges at Athleague, Castlecoote and Castlestrange, and a study of the map will suggest how the route could be short-cut at Castlestrange if required.

Introduction

The River Suck has attracted fishermen for decades, but it is only in recent years that the riverbanks have been promoted for walking. The Suck Valley is prime cattle country and there is good pasture available alongside the river. Local farmers have offered access through their

A ruined castle beside the River Suck at Athleague

fields and alongside the river to enable walkers to appreciate this gentle, green, low-lying countryside. There are plenty of signposts, waymark posts, stiles and footbridges where they are needed, but bear in mind that the river bursts its banks every winter and rising water levels can impinge on the path. If you choose to walk this route in the winter, it is a good idea to ask local people about the extent of flooding.

Looking back into the Suck Valley's distant past, there is a peculiar item of note; a boulder carved with flowing spiral designs at Castlestrange. The boulder is granite, and is likely to have been deposited in the area during the Ice Age. The designs carved on it are from the 'La Tène' period, dating back over 2,000 years. There are only two other stones like it in Ireland and doubtless they had some religious or ritual significance.

There are a few ruined castles in this part of the Suck Valley, and the local placenames point to a couple of them. When you start the walk at Athleague you'll see a castle near the bridge. This dates from the 14th century and was built by the O'Conors, the same ancient Irish clan who built the castle at Ballintober on another part of the Suck Valley Way. At Castlecoote there is little to see of the old castle, which the Coote family plundered as a source of stone when building themselves another house in the 18th century. Castlestrange is partly in ruins, with the ivy-clad remains of Captain Le Strange's 16th-century castle alongside a large house that was obviously once very grand. There were other fine houses in the locality, such as Rookwood House, of which very little trace remains, though it survived into the 1950s.

The Walk

This walk uses the Suck Valley Way from Athleague to Rookwood, then takes to minor roads to reach Castlecoote. The Suck Valley Way is used from Castlecoote to Castlestrange and so back to Athleague.

1. You can park near the bridge at Athleague, either beside the Bridge House or at an old church now used as an Angling Centre. If the Angling Centre is open, you'll find it offers plenty of information about the area. Start walking from the Bridge house, following a road signposted as the Suck Valley Way and Green Heartlands Cycle Route. Watch for a Suck Valley Way signpost on the right, and cross a stile to follow waymark posts through fields **(15mins)**.

   In summer, you may feel you are far from the river, but in winter it rises all the way to the waymarks. The seasonal flooding makes the river into a shallow lake, attracting ducks, geese, swans, curlew and snipe.

2. Follow the route in a straight line, crossing stiles as required to

pass from field to field, until you are drawn along a hedged track that can be muddy underfoot. Turn left along a narrow farm road flanked by low limestone walls and lush green fields. Turn left at a road junction, and the road later swings right. At the next road junction the Suck Valley Way turns left, but you should leave it and walk straight onwards to cross Rookwood Bridge. There are nine stone arches spanning the River Suck at this point **(1hr)**.

3. The road rising from the bridge is known locally as the Dark Road because of the trees that overhang it. The road passes a gatehouse cottage, now used for self-catering holidays, that is one of the few reminders of the old Rookwood estate. Look out for old iron gates and stout gate pillars. Follow the road to a crossroads and turn right **(1hr 30mins)**.

4. The road passes through a wetland area featuring some straggly woodland and patchy coniferous plantations. If you keep a careful eye on your map you'll notice a drainage ditch marks the county boundary as you pass from Co Galway to Co Roscommon. The road passes a few farmhouses and there are large fields used for sheep grazing. You reach another crossroads, where you walk straight onwards along the R366 **(2hrs 15mins)**.

5. The road passes more houses and fields, and there is a pronounced bend where the road passes an area that it spiky with rushes. Continue straight through another crossroads and the road leads you into the village of Castlecoote. You pass St. Kieran's Church, which has a car park and picnic benches opposite. Golden's Bar is passed later, and the Castlecoote Stores are reached beside Castlecoote Bridge **(3hrs 15mins)**.

    You are back on the Suck Valley Way at Castlecoote and if you'd like to take a break for lunch, then the timing includes an hour spent at this point. If you aren't carrying any food, you can obtain some from the stores.

6. Cross the seven-arched stone bridge to leave Castlecoote. The bridge has a modern top, but you can see the old stonework underneath. Steps lead down to the right and you follow a grassy embankment parallel to the river. After passing a large barn you later cross a small footbridge. The area known as Goat's Island is low-lying and readily floods, in which case you may find it necessary to skirt round the water keeping to the left. Waymark posts and stiles show the way along a brow overlooking the river and views stretch from Castlecoote to Castlestrange and Mount Mary.

    Walk from stile to stile to pass through the fields and the route eventually runs down on the low ground near the river again. In wet weather the ground can be muddy. Walk through a narrow belt of conifers, then continue towards the ivy-clad ruin of

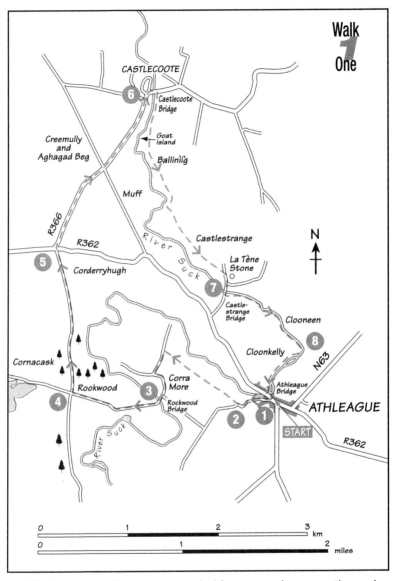

Castlestrange. Keep an eye peeled for waymark posts, stiles and a footbridge, then keep well to the right of the buildings to reach the access track at four big beech trees **(5hrs 30mins)**.

Take a break at this point to study the peculiar carved stone beneath the beeches. It has been surrounded with a grid to keep farm animals from rubbing against it. A notice alongside offers a few words about the stone, but its use has been long forgotten. It is over 2,000 years old and the style of its decoration is known as 'La Tène'.

7. Follow the track down to a gatehouse and walk straight across Castlestrange Bridge. There are many arches over the River Suck, but they can't be counted as there is a lot of tree scrub on an island in the middle. Turn left down some wooden steps, then follow the river downstream, crossing little footbridges over drainage ditches and stiles over fences. The land is green and grassy, low-lying and prone to seasonal flooding. Follow the river past a rickety old bridge **(6hrs)**.

8. As you follow the River Suck round a bend, the banks become rather wild and woody for a while, and parts of the path can be muddy. As you approach Athleague, there is a short, firm, dry path leading past the Angling Centre and returning you to the bridge where you started **(6hrs 30mins).**

    Note the old mills and the mill wheel across the river, as well as the ruins of an old castle. If the Angling Centre is open you may be able to pop in for refreshments, otherwise you can cross the bridge and obtain food and drink from the Bridge House.

Other walks in the area

The area is low-lying and the main access off-road is provided by the Suck Valley Way. Obtain a copy of the Suck Valley Way Map Guide locally and you can enjoy the southern parts of the route around Athleague, Ballygar and Creggs.

Places of interest

The countryside is full of ruins. You see old castles on the walk, and if you travel further afield you can see even more. Visit Roscommon Town to have a look at Roscommon Castle and Roscommon Abbey, both of which were founded in the 13th century.

Walk 2:
Ballymoe & Ballintober
Lovely low-lying landscape

The Suck Valley Way is a fine lowland walking route. It describes an elongated circuit and explores the countryside on either side of the River Suck. The loop around the northern end of the route makes a fine day's walk. You'll see no hills and mountains, no great lakes, and no dramatic scenery. Instead you'll be able to enjoy a lovely lowland countryside of green fields, along with a wild, heathery bog and gentle riverside paths. There are several points of historical interest along the way including a castle and an interesting heritage centre at Ballintober.

Grade: Easy

Distance: 26km (16 miles)

Time: 7½ hours (including an hour for lunch)

Start & Finish: Ballymoe 696718

Maps: Ordnance Survey of Ireland Discovery 39 & 40

How to get there
> *By car:* Ballymoe is between Roscommon and Castlerea on the main N60 road. Parking is available along the main street.
> *By bus:* Bus Éireann table number 21 is a daily service to Ballymoe from Dublin and Westport. Table number 429 is a less frequent service from Galway and Castlerea. Table number 457 is a Wednesday only service from Roscommon and Ballina.

Necessities: Boots as the ground can be wet and muddy; **waterproofs** if rain is forecast as there is little shelter; **money** for food and drink at Ballymoe or Ballintober.

Notes: This is an easy low-level walk along the well-waymarked Suck Valley Way. However, it is also quite a long walk, and if you a relying on the buses then you need to be in the right places at the right times. The full circuit is based on the village of Ballymoe, but you could also walk from Ballymoe to Castlerea and get the bus back, or walk from Ballymoe to Ballintober and arrange to be collected, rather than follow roads to complete the circuit.

Introduction

The Suck Valley Way is one of the best low-level waymarked trails in Ireland. Local farmers have provided access to their fields on a scale unknown elsewhere in the country. As the route runs from one field to another, you'll find stiles across walls and fences. When rivers and drainage ditches are crossed, you'll find footbridges. To keep you on course there are plenty of signposts and waymarks, as well as thoughtful extras such as picnic benches at intervals when you might like to take a break.

The northern loop of the Suck Valley Way runs from Ballymoe to

Ballintober, passing close to Castlerea on the way. A circuit is easily formed by closing the loops with a road walk at the end. The terrain is always low-level in gently rolling countryside. The landscape is mostly a patchwork of fields, providing pasture for sheep and cattle, but there are also wild, heathery raised bogs and small patches of forest. The Suck Valley Way occasionally runs alongside the River Suck, which is a noted angling river.

There are some interesting historical features along the way, including the shattered High Crosses at Emlagh and the mouldering castle ruins at Ballintober. An old National School at Ballintober has been made into a museum, You'll see a ruined church, abandoned farmhouses, old stone bridges and even a ruined railway station. You can use Ordnance Survey maps to complete this walk, or you could use the Suck Valley Way Map Guide, which shows much more detail of the route; even to the extent of showing every field boundary along the way.

The Walk

Start in Ballymoe, which is only just on the Co Galway side of the River Suck. If you need any food for your lunch, then there are a handful of small foodstores to hand. Unless you are prepared to move off-route to Castlerea, you won't be able to buy anything else until you reach Ballintober.

1. Leave Ballymoe by following the N60 road signposted for Castlerea. It is also signposted for the Suck Valley Way. The road crosses the Island River, which is a tributary of the River Suck. When the road bends right, follow a farm track on the left, passing a barn. Keep following the track as it bears to the right, then cross a stile and walk alongside an old drainage ditch and an electric fence. Keep following the ditch and fence until you can turn right, crossing two footbridges to reach a minor road (**20mins**).

2. Turn right along the road, then left at a house, and follow a track that is flanked by gorse bushes, offering good cover for pheasants. The track drifts to the right and there are views across Cooliskea Bog, which is a wild, heathery raised bog. Turn left at a junction of bog roads, then right at another junction. Enjoy the extensive views, where farms and fields suddenly seem very distant, and take note of the deep turf cuttings in the bog. Turn left at another junction of bog roads and walk until you reach a footbridge on the right (**50mins**).

3. Cross the footbridge and walk along an embankment between turf cuttings. Turn left and a fine grassy track leads onwards, eventually becoming flanked by gorse bushes and tree scrub. Another junction of bog roads is reached at a picnic bench. Turn right and

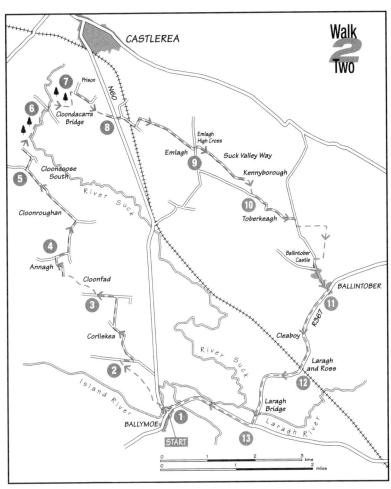

follow a track which itself turns left and right before reaching a narrow road **(1hr 10mins)**.

4. Turn right along the road, then left and straight on as waymarked. The road passes a couple of little houses, runs through a small beechwood, then passes a tiny roadside shrine before reaching a road junction. Turn left to follow a road past a few more houses. There is a bendy stretch where an old stone bridge is crossed. Hooded crows are often seen among the trees and fields. Watch for a turning on the right, along a narrower road **(1hr 40mins)**.

5. Follow the road towards a house and drift left along a track. A stile on the right leads into a field that slopes down towards the River Suck. Turn left to walk upstream, crossing little footbridges over inflowing drainage ditches. There is a young conifer plantation

beside the river, while ahead you can see the four stone arches of Cloondacarra Bridge **(2hrs 10mins)**.

6. Cross the bridge over the River Suck, then walk only a short way upstream on the other bank. Cross a footbridge over a sizeable inflowing drainage ditch, and follow that upstream instead. You can see the imposing structure of Castlerea Prison ahead, and the route is later signposted towards it, following a rugged ride through a young conifer plantation that gives way to an older stand of birch to reach a corner of the prison wall **(2hrs 30mins)**.

    You'll want to stop for lunch at some point, and this place is as good as any for a picnic. The time allowed for completing this walk assumes you'll take an hour's break around this point.

    Castlerea is signposted as being 500 metres away along a road, but in fact you could easily double that distance to reach the centre of town. There are plenty of places offering food and drink if you want to make the detour. If you decide to go into town for lunch, then allow yet another extra hour to walk there and back.

7. Follow the Suck Valley Way parallel to the prison wall, along a sort of grassy avenue with trees on either side. After passing the far corner of the prison wall you cross a stile and the way ahead can be muddy underfoot. When you reach a gateway, turn right to cross a stile and enter a coniferous forest **(3hrs 45mins)**.

    Follow a muddy forest ride, then turn left along a firm, narrow path between the tall and densely planted trees. The path reaches the main N60 road, where you should cross with care and turn left to reach a travellers' halting site **(4hrs)**.

    Travellers generally live in caravans and councils are obliged to provide halting sites for them. While their lifestyle may have some similarities with Gypsies, they are not related. Travellers in Ireland are ethnically Irish, although they have evolved a tradition and culture of their own. You will see metalwork items such as old cooking pots and bedsteads on sale by the roadside; items that are far too heavy for your rucksack!

8. Turn right off the main road opposite the halting site and follow a track. The track bends to the right and crosses the Dublin to Westport railway line at a level crossing. Continue walking to a house and turn left, then right, along another track. Follow the track up a gentle slope and you'll have wider and wider views across the gently rolling landscape. There are no houses beside the track at first, but there are later. Look out on the left for the remains of the High Crosses at Emlagh **(4hrs 15mins)**.

    A monastery once stood at Emlagh, but very little is known about its history. It was associated with St. Patrick, but the only remaining traces are the eight shattered pieces of two medieval High Crosses mortared into a huddle in the field.

9. Continue along the farm road to a junction with a minor road. Turn left, then right, to pass a stable and a few houses. The road becomes a track flanked by hedgerows and trees, ending at a gate. Cross a stile and keep to the right following markers pointing the way through three more fields to reach a narrow road. Turn left and follow this bendy road down to a junction with another road **(5 hrs)**.

10. Turn right along the road, then left to cross a stile beside a gate. Follow a rampant hedgerow away from the road, eventually turning right to follow the course of a drystone wall leading back towards the road. Turn left to follow the road into the village of Ballintober **(5hrs 30mins)**.

A tower on the ruined O'Conor castle at Ballintober

You'll notice a ruined, ivy-grown castle off to the right on entering Ballintober. This dates from 1322 and was once the seat of the O'Conor Don, though it was later used by Cromwellian troops.

Walking through Ballintober, you pass the Post Office and Smokie Joe's bar and restaurant. There is an interesting restored Holy Well off to the right, while the old National School in the village, on the left, has been converted to a museum. If you take a break to visit the museum, then you need to allow extra time for it. Further on through the village there is a wide green, church, a couple of grocery shops and Kenny's Bar at a crossroads.

11. Turn right at the crossroads to follow the R367 road uphill signposted for Ballymoe. The road is overhung by tall beeches for a while, then there are views across broad, rolling fields. Look out for an old Edward VIII postbox built into a wall just after passing Cleaboy House. The road crosses a bridge over the Dublin to Westport railway **(6hrs 20mins)**.

As you cross the bridge, you can see the old railway station and water tower; relics of the age of steam. Note that the fences beside the road have been made exclusively from old railway lines!

12. Lush sheep grazing pastures give way to damp and rushy fields beside the River Suck. Cross a low bridge over the Laragh River and walk to a junction with the main N60 road. Note that there is another old Edward VII postbox across the road **(6hrs 40mins)**.

13. Turn right as signposted for Ballymoe. As the road is busy, walk on the hard shoulder or grassy verge on the right, facing oncoming traffic. The road runs straight past the old Drumatemple National School, then later bends left to cross the River Suck and reach Ballymoe **(7hrs 30mins)**.

Have a look at the Garda Station on the right, where a plaque records the birth of Eamonn Kent on 21st September 1881. Kent was one of the signatories of the Proclamation of Independence in 1916. To the left of the road is an old Church of Ireland, with a pinnacled tower. It is worth having a look round the back of the churchyard, where you'll find the ornate tomb of the Bagot family.

If you're looking for food and drink, then the first bar you reach in Ballymoe is Joyce's Bar, though there are other bars along the road.

Other walks in the area

The area is low-lying and the main access off-road is provided by the Suck Valley Way. Obtain a copy of the Suck Valley Way Map Guide locally and you can enjoy the middle parts of the route around Glinsk, Donamon and Castlecoote.

Places of interest

Castlerea is the town nearest to this part of the Suck Valley Way. Nearby Clonalis House is the seat of the O'Conor Don, a direct descendant of the last High King of Ireland. It is a 19th-century house, signposted from the main roads.

Walk 3:
Ballyfarnon, Moytura & Geevagh
The Battle of Moytura

Moytura is the 'Plain of the Pillars' and the area is notable for the great number of archaeological remains scattered around the countryside. Moytura is also famous in Irish mythology as one of the most important battlegrounds in the country. The Battle of Moytura was fought between the divine Tuatha De Danann and the demonic Formorians. The powers of the main protagonists were awesome. The Formorian Balor of the Baleful Eye, could slay with a single glance from his evil eye. The Danann Lugh, easily identified as a solar deity, was a remarkably gifted leader. The carnage during the battle was colossal, and it is through the battlefield you walk as you explore Moytura.

Grade: Easy

Distance: 21km (13 miles)

Time: 7 hours (including an hour for lunch)

Start & Finish: Ballyfarnon 866137.

Maps: Ordnance Survey of Ireland Discovery 25 and Ordnance Survey of Northern Ireland Discoverer 26

How to get there
By car: Ballyfarnon is a village on the R284 road between Sligo city and Carrick-on-Shannon. You could also reach it from the main N4 road from Boyle, navigating a network of minor roads around Lough Key.
By bus: There are no bus services to Ballyfarnon.

Necessities: Boots as some parts can be muddy; **walking shoes** would suffice most of the time; **waterproofs** if rain is forecast**; food and drink** as there is little along the way; **money** for a drink at Geevagh or Ballyfarnon.

Notes: This is a relatively easy walk taking in part of the Miner's Way and Historical Trail, with other minor roads used to create a circuit via the village of Geevagh. Although a couple of parts can be quite muddy, most of the route is on firm, dry surfaces.

Introduction

The Battle of Moytura was some fight! Although the Tuatha De Danann and the Formorians are regarded as separate races, there were relations between them. Bres, who was king of the Dananns, had a Formorian father, and even the great champion Lugh was actually the grandson of Balor of the Baleful Eye. To appreciate the Battle of Moytura to any extent, you would have to read up a host of associated tales. The Dananns were brought to Ireland in a magical mist and conquered a race known as the Firbolgs before taking on the might of the Formorians.

Magic and mystery surround these ancient tales, and there are sev-

Following the Old Coach Road between Ballyfarnon and Highwood

eral curious events along the way. The great Danann known as the Dagda had a sexual union with the war goddess called the Morrigan beside Lough Arrow, gaining valuable support while battle plans were being laid. Lugh spent a considerable time interviewing all the Danann champions so that he could use their expertise to the full. Balor, the Formorian champion, could slay armies of men with a single glance from his evil eye. So sure of victory is Balor, that he'd already made plans for his ships to tow Ireland northwards into the Arctic after battle! The Dananns, meanwhile, had a magical well at their disposal, where any slain warrior could be revived to fight again!

Soon after the start of the battle, the Formorians filled the magical well with stones to deny the Dananns the chance to revive their warriors. When the carnage increased, the might of the armies and magical incantations wrought horrible destruction on both sides. At a pivotal moment in the battle, Balor opened his evil eye to strike the Dananns once more, but Lugh cast a sling stone through it. The last thing the eye did as Balor died was to burn a hole in the ground that can be seen to this day at Lough Nasool. The Formorians were driven into the sea, although one of them was spared to teach the Dananns a skill that they were entirely lacking; agriculture!

The walk takes in an old coach road from Ballyfarnon to Hightown, then wanders through the ancient, ritual landscape of Moytura. You'll be able to see some of the ancient monuments that cover the countryside, as well as enjoying extensive views for very little effort. Minor roads lead down to the little village of Geevagh, and from there you can link with a section of the Miner's Way to return to Ballyfarnon.

The Walk

There is a monument to a musician in the middle of Ballyfarnon, as well as parking spaces around the village. There are shops and bars if you need any food or drink before leaving.

1. Walk downhill from the monument in the middle of Ballyfarnon. The R284 road crosses the Feorish River and leaves the village. Turn left along a minor road that is signposted for the Miner's Way, Lough Arrow and Boyle. Turn right along another narrow road signposted only for the Miner's Way, and you'll reach another signpost and an information board where the Miner's Way and Historical Trail join together (**30mins**).

2. Walk straight along the track signposted as the Historical Trail. This is also known as the Old Coach Road, and there is a very muddy stretch in a dip. The continuation is rather narrower and generally grassy. When you reach a house, walk straight through a crossroads to continue along a narrow tarmac road. When the road bends right, you should bear left along another track (**1hr**).

3. As the track climbs, there are increasingly extensive views across the countryside. There is a steep-sided, wooded hollow off to the left, while in the rugged fields to the right is a megalithic tomb. Follow the track over a broad rise and then walk downhill. Cross over a minor road and continue down another short track, then turn right along another road (**1hr 20mins**).

4. Follow the road a short way, then turn left along a broad track signposted as the Historical Trail. The track passes a couple of houses and a couple of attractive little loughs, known as White Lough and Black Lough. When you reach a junction with a minor road, turn right and follow it uphill. Turn left at a crossroads at the top to pass the church and the old National School at Highwood (**2hrs**).

    Off to the right of the road is a prominent boulder known as the Eglone Stone. It is a glacial erratic, one of many in the locality, but its size and shape make it quite noticeable. Folklore says it was thrown here by a giant called Eglone, or that he lies buried beneath it. It is also said that beacon fires were lit on top of the stone at certain times of the year.

5. Follow the road away from Highwood to reach a junction beside a large modern house. The Historical Trail goes into fields above the road at this point for a short while, but if you turn right along a narrow road, you'll be able to have a look at a rather fine court tomb on the right. There are also more glacial erratics scattered around the fields. The tomb has a little gate and path leading to it, and afterwards you can continue along the road to rejoin the His-

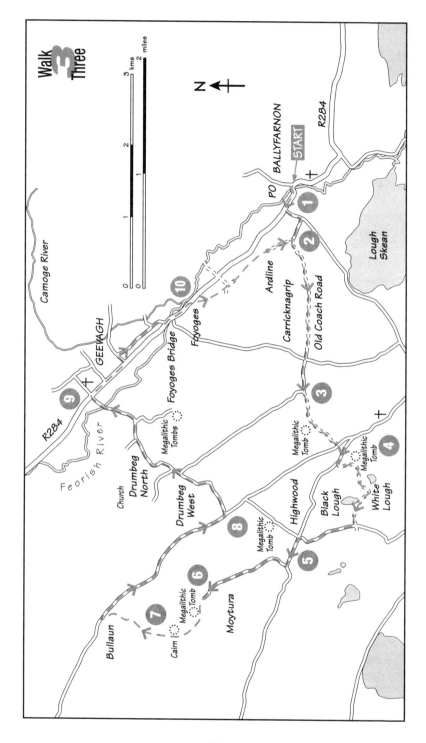

torical Trail and walk to the farm at the end of the road (**2hrs 30mins**).

6. Watch for waymark posts to pass to the left of a large tank. The markers will lead you through high, rugged fields, but off to the right is another portal tomb you might want to see. The waymarked route leads through little gates until you reach a trig point at 226m (741ft) with a fine view across Moytura (**2hrs 45mins**).

Looking round at the view, you can see the Bricklieve Mountains, Ox Mountains and Knocknarea. You can also see beyond the Castlegal Range, and round to the broad slopes of the Arigna Mountains, as well as across the lowland plains. The area is crowded with ancient monuments, maybe a greater concentration than elsewhere in Ireland.

A large rock near the trig point is said to be where Lugh sat and commanded the Danann forces in their battle against the Formorians. When Balor of the Baleful Eye was slain, his final glance burnt a hole in the ground where Lough Nasool now lies. If you were to continue along the course of the Historical Trail, you'd reach a megalithic tomb known as the Labby Rock, which has a monstrous capstone.

In fine weather this is a good place to break for lunch, and the time allowance for the walk assumes you'll spend an hour at this point.

7. To descend from the hill, walk roughly northwards down towards some houses. You pass a hillside well, then go through gates and follow a farm access road away from the buildings. When you reach a junction with a minor road beside a forest, turn right and follow the road as it climbs very gently uphill to a junction (**4hrs**).

8. Turn left to follow another minor road, which drops downhill and twists and turns on its way to the little village of Geevagh. Halfway downhill, look out on the left and you'll see a ruined church on a little hill. At the bottom of the road you cross the Feorish River on a three-arched stone bridge. Turn right on the R284 road at Geevagh Cross. There is a shop and a pub if you need food or drink at this point (**5hrs**).

9. Follow the R284 road away from Geevagh Cross, then turn left along a minor road signposted for St. Eilbhe's Well. Follow the road only a short way, then turn left along a narrower road signposted for the Miner's Way. This old road leads back to the busier R284 road, where you cross Foyoges Bridge over the River Feorish (**5hrs 30mins**).

Note the waterwheel beside the river, which now generates electricity for Annagh Lodge.

10. After crossing Foyoges Bridge, watch for a signpost on the right, where the old road continues as a rough track flanked by trees. The surface can be muddy in places, but the course of the old track is always clear. Simply follow it back to the signpost indicating both the Miner's Way and Historical Trail that you passed earlier in the day's walk. All you need to do to complete the walk is turn left and left again along minor roads, then right along the R284 road to return to Ballyfarnon, food and drink (**6hrs 30mins**).

Other walks in the area

The Historical Trail provides the main off-road access in the area. Obtain a copy of the Miner's Way & Historical Trail Map Guide and you can explore other parts of the route around Lough Arrow and Lough Key, or link with the Miner's Way over Kilronan Mountain.

Places of interest

The area is rich in archaeology and you could spend days with a map wandering around ancient tombs and standing stones. The Labby Rock and Heapstown Cairn are worth visiting near Lough Arrow.

Walk 4:
The Arigna Mountains
The Miner's Way

There are very few places in Ireland where workable deposits of coal occur, but one of the most important sites was in the Arigna Mountains. Seams were thin and as a consequence, mining was hard. In the end, the industry ceased to be economical and the mines closed. The Miner's Way explores the post-industrial landscape and the high points of Corrie Mountain and Kilronan Mountain are covered on this walk in a circuit from the village of Arigna.

Grade: Moderate

Distance: 26km (16 miles)

Time: 9 hours (including an hour for lunch)

Start & Finish: The Miner's Arms in Arigna 930142

Map: Ordnance Survey of Northern Ireland Discoverer 26

How to get there

> *By car:* Arigna is near the southern end of Lough Allen and is served by a network of minor roads. It can be approached from Drumshanbo, Carrick-on-Shannon or Drumkeeran.
> *By bus:* There are no bus services to Arigna.

Necessities: Boots as the ground can be rough and wet; **waterproofs** as the uplands can be quite exposed; **food and drink** as there is nowhere to buy things en route.

Notes: The Miner's Way forms the basis for this walk in the Arigna Mountains. The route is waymarked and there are alternatives that allow shorter circuits to be followed. If you feel the walk is too long, then make use of the alternatives. The full route takes in bleak moorlands that were once mined for coal and now support windfarms.

Introduction

The Arigna Mountains are made of sandstone and shale, along with thin seams of coal. The coal was mined by a variety of methods, from the sinking of small-scale pits to large-scale open cast mining. There was only one townland, Derreenavogey, where individual farmers owned the mineral rights and operated tiny mines. They were often in dispute with each other, digging too far sideways and removing their neighbours' coal! The coal that was mined in this way was either for use on the farm, or if there was excess, it was taken to market along with all the other farm produce.

On most of Corrie Mountain the mineral rights were held by the owners of Kilronan Castle, and a company held a licence to work the coal, employing local people. There were plenty of small pits, and as the coal seams were very thin, conditions inside the mines were very cramped, with only limited mechanisation. Commercially mined coal from these pits was generally used by the Arigna Power Station on the shores of Lough Allen. Later, it became more economic to strip the surface off the mountain and remove the coal by open-cast mining. Landowners were compensated as the last reserves of coal were worked. Mining finally ceased in 1990, and the coal-fired Arigna Power Station closed soon afterwards.

Today there has been a remarkable turnaround in the area. Following the closure of the Arigna Power Station, measurements taken on Corrie Mountain and Kilronan Mountain suggested that the open moorlands might be suitable for windfarms. Consequently, two sites were established, each with ten huge turbines. Local people decided to capitalise on the memory of the recent mining industry by creating the Miner's Way. This route links some of the old mining sites and traverses the quiet countryside between them. There are also plans to establish a mining museum above the village of Arigna, and there is no shortage of artefacts in the surrounding countryside waiting to be put on display.

This walk is based on a loop of the Miner's Way, based on the village of Arigna, climbing to Corrie Mountain and Kilronan Mountain in a long circuit. There are minor roads and alternative paths if you'd prefer a shorter walk. There are also walking festivals in the area, usually held in May and October, when you could walk with knowledgeable local walkers, and even some of the former miners, and hear of their love for the area.

The Walk

If you can navigate along minor roads to Arigna, then you'll have no problem following the waymarked Miner's Way afterwards. Park near the Miner's Arms beside the bridge over the Arigna River. There is a shop alongside if you need food or drink for your lunch.

1. Leaving the Miner's Arms, follow the road uphill towards the Arigna Fuels plant, identified by its smoking chimney. It makes compressed briquettes from imported coal slack, so the coal industry isn't quite finished in the area. Turn right where a marker post points you along another road up to the church. Continue up a steep road above the church, passing a graveyard to reach another road junction. Turn right here, then look out for a battered old mining track on the left **(30mins)**.

2. The rugged track climbs steeply to a gate, and continues uphill as a broken concrete road. Turn right and cross a stile by a gate, where there is a Miner's Way signpost and a marker post. There is no doubting that it has been uphill work all the way, but now there's an easier interlude. The route follows a gritstone terrace, crossing several stiles over fences, following marker posts throughout.

This is Derreenavogey, where the farmers living at the foot of the

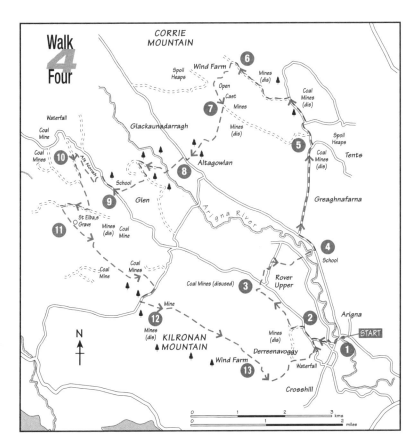

slope worked their own little mines. Note the old pylons that once supported an aerial ropeway carrying coal down from the higher commercial mines. There are fine views over Lough Allen to Corrie Mountain and Slieve Anierin.

When you pass a ruined building, look inside to see the remains of the old leather bellows. This was a forge connected with the mines. The route continues towards the prominent spoil heap of the Rover Mine. Walk down a track and pass the abandoned 'hutches' – the local name for the little metal trucks that ran along rails to transport coal out of the mines. A minor road is joined below (**1hr**).

3. Turn quickly right and left to cross the road, then follow a path marked by a signpost to continue across the valley. Zig-zag down a rocky edge and walk through a squelchy field, then turn right to reach a gate and another minor road. Turn left down the road, then right as signposted to walk through more squelchy fields. An access road leads down to another minor road, which you cross to

continue. Steps and a riverside path lead to a footbridge and more steps, Climbing to the Greaghnafarna School **(1hr 30mins)**.

4. The Miner's Way is indicated as turning right along the road, but to continue with this walk, you should turn left instead, following a signpost for the Doon Loop. The road makes a dip, then you turn right up another minor road, climbing straight up a slope of poor farmland. There is an attractive thatched cottage on the way, and the higher ground is damp and spiked with rushes. Follow the road gently downhill past patchy forestry plantations to reach a junction called the Seltanaskeagh Crossroads **(2hrs 15mins)**.

    This area is also known as Tents, receiving that name during the 1798 Rebellion, when a French army camped on the mountainside. They were later defeated at Ballinamuck.

5. Turn left at the junction to walk through a patch of forest, then turn left again up a rather battered road, signposted as the Miner's Way. The ground is rushy and heathery moorland, with a little tree scrub. Yet another left turn is signposted, leading up a stony track that once served a series of mines. There are spur tracks to right and left, but don't follow any of them. There is a sizeable spoil heap off to the left, known as Spion Kop. Keep straight on as indicated, through a gate, with a good view off to the right **(3hrs)**.

    The view takes in Lough Allen, which is the first of many fine loughs along the course of the River Shannon. Mountains in view are ranged around the horizon from Truskmore and the Darty Mountains to Cuilcagh, The Playbank and Slieve Anierin.

6. Follow the track across the upper slopes of Corrie Mountain, turning left along a track, through another gate and passing some of the towering turbines. You'll see a prominent old mine building, which offers the only shelter on these exposed uplands. Turn left again and follow the road downhill. A broad track aims for the village of Arigna, identified from afar by the smoking chimney of the Arigna Fuels plant. The slopes have been devastated by open cast mining and are wild and rugged. Watch carefully for a marker post pointing downhill to the right **(3hrs 30mins)**.

    There is a pleasant view from the moorland slopes of Corrie Mountain, so this is as good a place as any for lunch. The time allowance for the walk includes an hour spent here.

7. Follow a drainage ditch straight down a broad, boggy, heather moorland slope. A sign points to the left, indicating the Doon Loop if you'd prefer a shorter walk, otherwise continue downhill. Drift to the right, cross a stile over a fence, then turn right to reach a forest. Walk straight downhill on a grassy ride through the forest, continuing down to a road and a farm on the valley side **(5hrs)**.

Coal mines in the Arigna Mountains were very cramped places

8. Turn right on the road, then left to walk down through fields to reach the Arigna River. Cross a metal footbridge and climb up steps, then head off to the right along a grassy forest ride. When you emerge in a clear-felled area, follow a forest track uphill. The track later swings sharply left, then you turn right up another track to leave the forest. Marker posts point the way up a steep slope, passing a couple of ruined houses and an old school to reach a disused church on a high road **(5hrs 30mins)**.

9. Turn right along the road and pass a house, then turn left and climb steeply uphill through a young forest. You are actually on an old mine incline where coal trucks, or 'hutches' were lowered downhill to the road. Turn left at the top of the incline and contour across the rugged moorland slope. Swing sharply right and rise gently across the next rugged heathery slope, eventually following a rocky edge called Alt Norah. Markers point the way ahead, then you turn left and follow a track uphill that is grassy in parts and quite rocky in others **(6hrs)**.

10. Turn left up another old mining track, which actually crosses tilted bedrock for a while. The area has been extensively mined, and you follow the track through a mini-canyon exposed by open-cast mining. The track continues along a low rocky edge above a bog, reaching a junction beside a ragged line of telegraph poles. Turn right here and follow a clearer track for a while, which later zig-zags downhill. A signpost on the left indicates a path to St.

Ailbhe's Well and the Kilronan Mountain Loop. The well is marked by a cross **(6hrs 45mins)**.

St. Ailbhe's Well is a curious place, and undoubtably the Holy Well is ancient. A slab of stone is said to mark the burial place of St. Ailbhe, which was the subject of a notable summer pilgrimage. The cross is relatively recent, and there are usually coins and assorted trinkets left there. Alongside is a drystone structure where sick people were left overnight on the mountainside in the hope that they would be cured of their ailments.

11. The path continues quite clearly across the moorland slopes and is nearly always wet underfoot. Follow the markers until you reach a prominent spoil heap, then aim for telegraph poles and join a track. Turn left to follow the track, passing through double gates. Join a tarmac road and turn right to pass a mast, continuing down a forested slope that has been clear-felled. Turn left along a track signposted for the Famine Grave, and you'll reach another ruined mining site. The pit had a large entrance and you can see an alcove where a statue of the Virgin once stood. The Famine Grave is along a gravel path in a forest. If you visit the place then you have to retrace your steps **(7hrs 45mins)**.

12. Follow the rather muddy track onwards, up and down in an area of young forest. Turn left along a grassy path, rising above the forest to follow markers up a gentle moorland slope to the turbines on top of Kilronan Mountain **(8 hrs)**.

13. Follow the road away from the turbines, and as it starts descending, look out for a marker pointing off to the left. A squelchy moorland path links with a track and proceeds gently downhill.

    Keep an eye peeled for another marker on the left, indicating another path leading more directly towards the village of Arigna. After crossing a stile, turn right and walk downhill beside an abandoned house. A stream, fence and tumbled wall lead downhill at first, then you drift to the left and eventually land on a minor road. Turn left up the road, then right to walk downhill to the church. Simply continue downhill through the village to return to the Miner's Arms **(9hrs)**.

Other walks in the area

The Miner's Way provides the main off-road access in the area, and the route described is a truncated version of the circuit. Obtain a copy of the Miner's Way & Historical Trail Map Guide and you can explore all parts of the route.

Places of interest

A mining museum is planned for the little village of Arigna, and when built this should be a focal point in the area, preserving the memory of the coal mining industry in the area.

Walk 5:
Glenade Arroo & Wild Cat's Hole
The Dartry Mountains

Broad and bleak heather moorlands characterise the higher parts of the Dartry mountains, but there are low outcrops of gritstone and little jewel-like loughs catch the eye. The lower slopes are limestone and there is a curious feature of note at the end, where the Wild Cat's Hole swallows a sizeable stream that flows from the high moorlands. On a clear day you could enjoy a lovely walk over these empty moorlands and delight in the open spaces, but in mist and rain you'd find little enjoyment and you'd have to complete the circuit by taking a series of compass bearings.

Grade: Moderate

Distance: 21km (13 miles)

Time: 7 hours (including an hour for lunch)

Start & Finish: Rassaun in Glenade 850445

Map: Ordnance Survey of Ireland Discovery 16

How to get there
> *By car:* The R280 road between Manorhamilton and Bundoran runs through Glenade, but you should actually follow a minor road running roughly parallel to it, on the opposite side of the Bonet River. About 1.5km (1 mile) after passing the church at Mullies, there is a prominent track heading off uphill to the right of the road. You need to find a space to park your car, then you're ready to walk.
> *By bus:* There are no bus services through Glenade. The nearest bus services are at Manorhamilton some 6km (4 miles) away.

Necessities: Boots as the high moorlands can be uneven and boggy; **waterproofs** as there is no shelter in rain; **compass** to assist with navigation even in clear weather; **food and drink** as there is nothing nearby.

Notes: It is a good idea to choose a fine day for your walk in the Dartry Mountains. The high moorlands are rough and pathless, though there are some paths and tracks on the lower slopes. If you're a good navigator with map and compass, then you might enjoy finding your way around these bleak moorlands in rain and mist, but it is more like a treadmill in those conditions.

Introduction

Hard, dark gritstone overlies lighter limestone beds in the Dartry Mountains. The underlying geology has an immediate effect on the shape of the landforms and on the vegetation cover. Glenade is a green valley with steep sides, and while Glenade Lough sits serenely in the middle of the valley, some of the streams flowing down from the mountains are swallowed into caves in the limestone. The higher Dartry Mountains are bleak, boggy and heathery, and the little lakes that sit on the moorland crest have no hope of draining into the hard bedrock.

You won't see many walkers on the Dartry Mountains, if any at all, but on a clear day you'll be able to revel in the open spaces and wander at will across the pathless heather moorlands.

Perched high on a broad moorland gap is a standing stone. Little is known about it, but it has been suggested to date from the Neolithic period. Although the wider area has plenty of archaeological remains, and there is an ancient cairn near the summit of Arroo, this is the only real feature of antiquity on the broad moorlands of the Dartry Mountains.

Of more recent times are a huddle of millstones that lie abandoned in the heather. They were carved out of the gritstone and were destined for a mill far below, but the mill went out of business and the stones were never taken down from the moorlands. They're not easy to locate, but if you follow the route directions and keep your eyes peeled, then you might find them.

The walk takes in the Wild Cat's Hole, which you won't find marked on the current Ordnance Survey maps. This is odd, because a preliminary edition of the map marked the waterfalls that plunge into the hole. Even odder, the old half-inch to one mile maps actually named the Wild Cat's Hole, even though space was at a premium. The hole swallows a river shortly after it pours over an impressive waterfall, and it is just one of a handful of features you'll find while walking over the Dartry Mountains.

A walk over the Dartry Mountains and Arroo usually features in the programme of walks organised for the North Leitrim Glens Walking Festival. The event is based on the nearby little town of Manorhamilton around Easter and October each year. Other popular routes take in the awesome pinnacles of Cloontyprughlish on the other side of Glenade, and parts of the waymarked Leitrim Way.

The Walk

Follow the directions given above to reach Rassaun in Glenade. Park carefully beside the road at Rassaun, taking care not to cause any kind of obstruction. You could always ask for permission to park off the road in a farmyard.

1. Start the walk by following a clear, enclosed track uphill from the minor road at Rassaun. The track runs north-eastwards and climbs gently at first, passing beneath two power lines. The track tists and turns on the steeper slopes and rises above the fields to peter out on a higher slope of turf cuttings. Walk north-eastwards again on the rugged moorland slopes, walking through pathless heather and boulders to reach a broad moorland summit at 423m (1,390ft). There are two little pools nearby, called Lough Agu and Lough Agow **(1hr 15mins)**.

Taking a break at one of the cairns on the heathery Dartry Mountains

2. Enjoy the views that have opened up in most directions, then face north-west towards the higher moorlands. The pool called Lough Nabrack fills a broad gap on the moorland crest and you walk gently downhill towards it. The ground is rather boggy and the firmest footing is found just beyond the outflow from the little lough **(1hr 30mins)**.

3. Walk along the broad moorland crest and gain height gradually on the heathery, bouldery slope. Looking ahead on a clear day, you'll see a cairn far ahead, and you should walk straight towards it. You'll find that there are plenty of cairns along the high crest, and some of them make fine viewpoints as the walk progresses. There is a very slight gap on the heathery crest, where you should drift more to the west to reach a summit at 482m (1,609ft) beside Lough Aganny **(2hrs 15mins)**.

4. As you walk further along the moorland crest, views open up well on either side, but looking northwards, the broad hump of Arroo limits the view. The high crest undulates gently and there are low outcrops of gritstone along the way.

Be sure to look carefully around the side of the low outcrops of gritstone, and you may spot a few huge millstones lying abandoned in the heather. They were hewn from the rock in situ and should finally have been rolled downhill to be transported to a mill, but the mill went out of business and the millstones were simply left high on the moors.

The lowest gap on the way to Arroo is easily determined as you pass a prominent little standing stone. If you happen to be following this walk in mist, then this feature makes a very useful reference point (**2hrs 30mins**).

5. Rise gently along the moorland crest and pass the pool of Arroo Lough. Continuing northwards, the slopes are rather more rugged and lead finally to the summit trig point on Arroo at 523m (1,720ft), where you can stop and observe the full extent of the view (**3 hrs**).

   Looking far to the north-west you can make out Slieve League and the Carrick Peninsula on a clear day, followed by the Blue Stack Mountains of Donegal, Breesy Hill and the Cliffs of Magho in Fermanagh. The Lough Navar and Big Dog Forests lead the eye to Belmore Mountain, Dough and Cuilcagh. Beyond Benbo rise the Arigna Mountains, followed by the hummocky crest of the Castlegal Range across Glencar. Truskmore and Tievebaun rise across Glenade, with a peep beyond at Mullaghmore Head by the sea.

   You might as well break for lunch on the summit of Arroo while there is the chance of a good view. The time allowance for the walk assumes you'll spend an hour at this point. In foul weather there is precious little shelter on the hill.

6. The return journey makes use of an obvious moorland shelf running all the way along the western slopes of the Dartry Mountains. In fact, it is always a good idea, on the outward journey, to keep casting an eye over the shelf, so that you're well aware of its presence and layout when you come to follow it. You should retrace your steps from the summit of Arroo to Arroo Lough first (**4hrs 20mins**).

7. Walk southwards from Arroo Lough to land on the moorland shelf, then keep to the gentle slopes with slightly steeper slopes above and below you. If you stick to this course, which is completely without trodden paths, then you'll cross a couple of small streams, as well as boggy areas and decaying blanket bog with awkward peat hags. Despite the awkward terrain in places, keep following the line of the moorland shelf to reach Cullionboy. At this point you should find a small, circular, drystone sheepfold perched on the edge of the shelf (**6hrs**).

   There is a good view down to Rassaun, where you started walking earlier in the day, and a splendid view of the rugged Castlegal Range beyond Glencar.

8. Descend slopes that are rather steeper and a bit more rugged to reach a river. This river flows from Lough Nabrack (which you passed earlier in the day), but you join it much further downstream. Follow the river downstream without crossing it, then

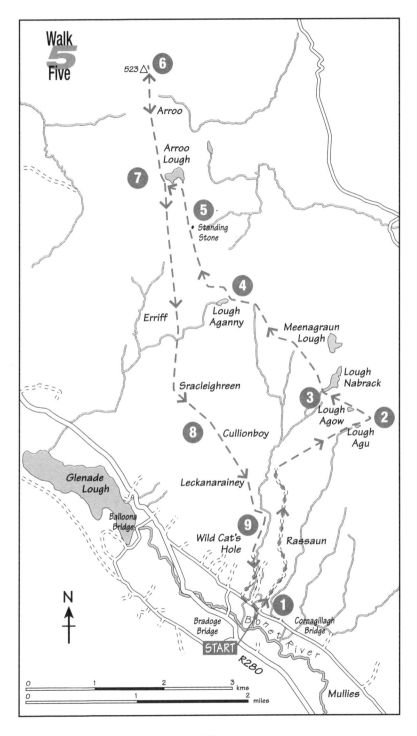

Walk
5
Five

523△ **6**

Arroo

Arroo
Lough

7

5
• Standing
Stone

4

Erriff

Lough
Aganny

Meenagraun
Lough

Sracleighreen

Lough
Nabrack

3
Lough
Agow

2

Lough
Agu

8   Cullionboy

Glenade
Lough

Leckanarainey

Balloona
Bridge

Wild Cat's
Hole

9

Rassaun

Bonet River

Cornagillagh
Bridge

N

Bradoge
Bridge

START

R280

Mullies

| 0 | 1 | 2 | 3 kms |

| 0 | 1 | 2 miles |

look out for a vague path which leads you onto a clearer track on the lower slopes. Follow the track, as the river is drawn into a rocky gorge ending with a sudden waterfall, so you can't follow it in that direction. However, once the track zig-zags down through the lower fields, you should make a short diversion into the wooded, rocky gorge to take a look at the waterfall (**6hrs 30mins**).

This is Wild Cat's Hole. The river pours over a lip of limestone into the wooded gorge and is well worth seeing, especially after heavy rain. If you look at the course of the river, you'll see that the water flows no great distance from the deep plunge pool beneath the waterfall before sinking into the riverbed. The water enters subterranean limestone passages and emerges further downstream to augment the water in the Bonet River.

9. Follow the track onwards, passing beneath two power lines, and pass derelict houses to reach a minor road at Rassaun. Turn left and walk past attractive farm cottages to return to your starting point (**7hrs**).

Other walks in the area

One of the most bizarre rock formations in Ireland can be studied by climbing up to Cloontyprughlish on the opposite side of Glenade. There is also a short, interesting waterfall walk by the Glenaniff River.

Places of interest

Manorhamilton has an interesting little town trail and many fine buildings. Hamilton's Castle dates from the 17th century. If you need information about the area, then call into the Glens Centre in Manorhamilton.

Walk 6:
Glencar & the Castlegal Range
A hummocky hill walk

The Castlegal Range lies on the south side of Glencar, between Sligo and Manorhamilton. It is a rugged little range of limestone hills, and some of the slopes on the Glencar side are quite steep and rocky. You could ask someone to drop you at one end of the range and collect you at the other, or you could start on the shore of Glencar Lough and enjoy an extended circuit taking in both the glen and the hills.

Grade: Moderate

Distance: 27km (17 miles)

Time: 9 hours (including an hour for lunch)

Start & Finish: Glencar Waterfall 760434

Map: Ordnance Survey of Ireland Discovery 16

How to get there
> *By car:* The main N16 road between Sligo and Manorhamilton runs through Glencar, and there are two minor roads signposted for Glencar Lough. There is a car park at the Glencar Waterfall at the eastern end of the lake.
> *By bus:* Bus Éireann table numbers 65, 66, 67 & 69 run along the Glencar road between Sligo and Manorhamilton. If you use these services and want to limit the amount of road-walking, then restructure the walk to start and finish on the main road and you could complete the walk along the Castlegal Range in 18km (11 miles).

Necessities: Boots as the ground can be rough, uneven and boggy in places; **waterproofs** as the hills can be exposed in wet weather; **food and drink** as there is nothing along the way; **compass** to navigate over the hills in mist.

Notes: The Castlegal Range is quite rough and knobbly, with plenty of little hills featuring short, steep slopes. There are only a few paths and in mist it can be a confusing place. The full circuit from Glencar Lough is quite long, but note how it can be shortened if you use the bus services through Glencar.

Introduction

Most people driving through Glencar find their gaze drawn to the lovely Glencar Lough, to the rocky slopes of King's Mountain, and to a curious waterfall that has a habit of curling back on itself whenever the wind blows. Few people turn their gaze to the rugged humps and bumps of the Castlegal Range; a chain of uneven limestone hills on the southern side of Glencar. In clear weather the range offers a splendid walk from end to end, but in mist it can be an awkward place for those whose navigational skills aren't up to scratch.

If you start this walk beside Glencar Lough, then you can study the rugged range from end to end and take note of the steep slopes flanking it. The walk starts by following roads, then climbs Leean Mountain first. After that there is a rugged roller-coaster ramble over Fawnlion, Hangman's Hill and Crockauns. There are paths and tracks in places, but they're not all going your way, and most parts are pathless and hummocky.

The last high point on the range is Cope's Mountain, then there is a descent to the main road. You follow roads back to Glencar Lough to finish the walk. You could, by judicious use of the bus services along the main road, omit most of the road-walking and simply tackle the best of the route over the high hills, between Diffreen and Castlegal. There are a couple of B&Bs near Glencar Lough and if you happen to use one of them as a base, then you can complete the circuit from the door after breakfast.

The Walk

The car park near Glencar Waterfall is the largest car park in Glencar. There are smaller ones close to the lake, but those are mainly used by fishermen. You might like to have a look at the waterfall before starting the walk.

1. Walk away from the Glencar Waterfall car park, following the minor road past Glencar Post Office. Continue straight on across the Diffreen River to join the main N16 road. Turn left and follow the road round a bend, crossing the Diffreen River again at Diffreen Bridge, passing Diffreen National School and Diffreen Cemetery **(1hr)**.

2. Turn right at the cemetery, leaving the main road and following a narrow farm road. You cross the Diffreen River one last time, then the road becomes quite patchy and is later no more than a gravel track. Turn left and left again to enter a forest at Gleneigh. The track climbs and passes a stone building with a corrugated iron roof. Continue climbing to reach a point where tracks cross, and turn left to leave the forest and emerge on a hillside **(1hr 30mins)**.

3. Go through a gate on the right, walking through a sheep-pen to start climbing up the slopes of Leean Mountain. Follow the edge of the forest uphill, climbing grassy and rushy slopes and crossing old turf cuttings. After crossing a fence, another slope of short grass leads further uphill, with the underlying limestone showing through. When you reach the top of Leean Mountain there is a trig point at 417m (1,373ft), which you'll only see when you're almost beside it **(2hrs)**.

Look westwards along the rugged crest of the Castlegal Range, where the summits are all shapes and sizes. You might as well take note of the terrain from afar, as you'll need to get quite involved in

Cope's Mountain seen from the floor of Glencar

route-finding as the walk progresses. In misty weather, however,
you'd be well to have your map and compass to hand at all times,
taking short bearings between summits and gaps throughout the
rest of the walk.

4. Descend a short, steep slope to the north-west, walking on grass
   and broken limestone. A fine grassy track runs across the slopes of
   Leean Mountain, but you simply step across it without following it
   anywhere. Keep well to the right of a sheep-pen to skirt a short
   rock-face on the far side of a little hill. Continue along a short,
   stony path to cross a broad and boggy area. Cross a fence on the
   gap and then climb straight up a short, steep, slope of grass on
   Fawnlion. There are two summits on this little hill, the highest
   being at 364m (1,200ft), and two low stone walls to cross **(2hrs
   30mins)**.

5. Walk over Fawnlion to reach a junction of fences, and follow a
   fence running downhill alongside a forest. A wall continues downhill from the forest, and there's a track alongside that you can
   follow for a while. The track actually leads downhill, away from
   the hills, so you should go through a gate on the right to continue.
   There are two little hills ahead, and you can either climb over both
   of them, or walk through a gap between them. To walk between
   them, cross a wall and a fence, then walk up through a dry valley
   between the hills. Another wall and fence run up through the

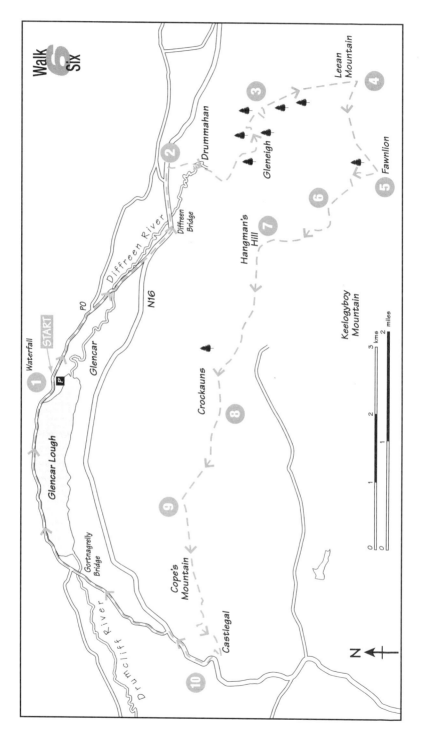

valley, and you can cross these on the narrow gap between the hills (**2hrs 45mins**).

6. To continue towards Hangman's Hill, contour around the steep slopes overlooking Gleneigh. You walk mostly on grass, but there are limestone outcrops too. As you contour round the hillside you'll be drawn into a small valley where you cross a stream. There is a grassy track on the other side of the stream and this leads up to a gateway in a fence. Beyond the gateway, turn right and cross a rough, heathery, boggy area, walking towards Hangman's Hill. Cross a fence before the slope steepens, then climb to the summit at 400m (1,310ft). The summit crest is a fine, heathery curve (**3hrs 15mins**).

   Looking back along the knobbly crest of the range, you'll notice Keelogyboy Mountain. This could have been included in the walk, but at the cost of extra effort and only by putting an awkward kink into the route. The crest of Hangman's Hill is a good enough place to break for lunch in fine weather, though in nasty weather you'd be advised to descend and seek a more sheltered spot. The time allowance for the walk assumes you'll take an hour's break at this point.

7. Be careful when you descend from Hangman's Hill, as there are outcrops of broken rock, but there are a couple of places where you can turn right and pass easily between the outcrops. Walk west across a broad, boggy, heathery gap, crossing a fence on the way. Looking ahead you'll see two hills rising beside each other. Both of them have lines of cliffs that can't be tackled by walkers, so aim for the little valley between the two hills, where you cross a fence near a small stream. Drift uphill to the right on a grassy slope, crossing a wall and fence on the way to Crockauns. There are small outcrops of limestone and low, ruined walls. The summit of Crockauns is marked by a cairn at 463m (1,527ft) and this is a good place to study the view (**5hrs 15mins**).

   Looking across Glencar you can admire King's Mountain and the broad-shouldered Truskmore. The Dartry Mountains fill the view to the north-east. You can look back to Hangman's Hill, Leean Mountain and Keelogyboy Mountain, and beyond to Slieve Anierin. The Arigna Mountains and Bricklieve Mountains are to the south, then the broad Ox Mountains and Nephin rise well to the west. Closer to hand is the prominent hump of Knocknarea.

8. Walk westwards from Crockauns, and a slope of grass and limestone outcrops gives way to a broad, boggy, heathery gap. You can follow a fence across the gap and it will lead you onto the rugged moorland crest of Cope's Mountain. The fence is off to one side of the crest and if you want to include the summit at 452m (1,487ft) then you should make a detour (**6hrs**).

9. In clear weather you'll be able to leave Cope's Mountain easily enough, but if the top is covered in mist then you should proceed with care, as there are unseen cliffs in most directions. Keep walking westwards and stay on the broad crest until you can follow a path through the heather. The path descends from the high heather slopes onto a steep grassy slope. The path becomes a fine and obvious track that zig-zags further downhill. On the lower slopes the track is lined with trees, and a gateway finally leads onto the main N16 road **(7hrs)**.

10. Turn right to walk along the main road, but only until you have walked round a couple of bends. Turn left along a minor road signposted for Glencar, following it downhill and crossing the Drumcliff River at the bottom. You reach the shore of Glencar Lough close to a B&B. It would be wonderful if there was a pleasant lakeshore path you could use at the end, but there is none, only a few access points for fishermen. Follow the road onwards, which is often flanked by trees that obscure a view across the lake. When the road moves away from the lake, it reaches the car park for the Glencar Waterfall and the walk is at an end **(9hrs)**.

Other walks in the area

Lough Gill in just to the south of the Castlegal Range, and the Sligo Way wanders along its southern shore before terminating at Dromahair. You can gaze on the 'Lake Isle of Inisfree' so beloved of the poet W. B. Yeats.

Places of interest

Parke's Castle on the northern shore of Lough Gill is worth a visit. It is a 17th-century fortified manor house in a particularly good state of preservation.

Walk 7:
King's Mountain & Benbulbin
'The Land of Heart's Desire'

William Butler Yeats, poet and stateman, lies buried in the shadow of Benbulbin. He had a particular affection for this part of Co Sligo, calling it 'the Land of Heart's Desire'. The sight of Benbulbin's proud prow from the road below is enough to make anyone with a soul to be stirred want to climb the mountain. A direct ascent is not recommended, but if you head round into Glencar you'll find a valley cut into the steep slopes of King's Mountain offers easy access.

Grade: Moderate

Distance: 19km (11 miles)

Time: 7 hours (including an hour for lunch)

Start & Finish: At Lislahelly near Drumcliffe 703426

Map: Ordnance Survey of Ireland Discovery 16

How to get there

By car: You can approach King's Mountain and Belbulbin from Sligo city by taking either of two main roads; the N15 coast road, or the N16 inland through Glencar. If you're on the coastal road, you can reach Lislahelly by following minor roads from Rathcormack. If you're on the Glencar road, then again, you can use minor roads to reach Lislahelly. Note that parking is extremely limited, so whatever approach you use, keep an eye peeled for a handy parking space.

By bus: Daily Bus Éireann services will get you within walking distance of Lislahelly, but they only operate along the main roads. Table number 480 is the local service along the coast road, though you could also use table numbers 64 or 69. On the Glencar road, table numbers 65, 66, 67 & 69 are useful services.

Necessities: Boots as the going can be rough and boggy on the uplands; **waterproofs** as the high ground can be exposed; **compass** in case of mist on high ground; **food and drink** as there is nothing on the walk.

Notes: The walk over King's Mountain and Benbulbin is relatively straightforward in good weather, but you should be aware that many parts are pathless and need careful navigation. In mist it is altogether more difficult to find your way around the boggy plateau, and there are dangerous cliffs on most sides that you should keep away from. Choose a clear day for the walk and you'll be rewarded with wonderful views.

Introduction

Anyone looking at King's Mountain and Benbulbin for the first time can be forgiven for not spotting any obvious ways to the top. The high plateau is fringed with cliffs and gullies, and the steep slopes are

A walker follows a path up the steep slopes of King's Mountain

strewn with scree. The lower slopes are divided up into small fields surrounded by walls, fences and hedgerows, so that all approaches look like obstacle courses. At Lislahelly, however, there is a path that's been in regular use for decades, rising through the fields, then zig-zagging across the steep slopes to enter a valley sliced through King's Mountain. In fact, this valley leaves King's Mountain with two summits, and you can visit one on the outward journey and the other on the return. Both of them feature good views.

With King's Mountain underfoot, all you need is good weather to enjoy a circuit around Benbulbin. Again, there are splendid views, as the mountain is literally out on a limb, overlooking an area of much lower ground stretching to the coast. It is countryside with a rich heritage, beloved by the poet Yeats, who lies buried at the foot of the mountain in the churchyard at Drumcliffe.

If you know anything about the complexities of copyright law, you might be interested to hear that the world's first copyright action took place in Ireland in the year 561, and culminated in the 'Battle of the Books' on the slopes below Benbulbin. St. Columbkille secretly copied a psalter belonging to St. Finian. The furious Finian demanded the copy, saying it rightly belonged to him, and in the end Columbkille was hauled before the High King of Ireland. Judgement was given in the following terms: 'To every cow its calf and to every book its copy.'

The book was ordered to be returned to Finian. In a fury, Columbkille's cousins, the O'Donnell's virtually declared war on the High King, and in the ensuing conflict, some 3,000 men were killed below Benbulben in the 'Battle of the Books'. Columbkille was again hauled before the High King. He was sent into exile and ordered to convert 3,000 heathens to replace the 3,000 slain men. This he duly accomplished on the Scottish island of Iona, where he was buried in 497.

The copy of the psalter became a prized possession of the O'Donnells of Donegal. They knew it as the 'Cathach' or 'Battle Book' and they carried it three times around their army before going into battle. This practice served them well until 1497, when they lost the book to the MacDermotts. The book is now in the care of the Royal Irish Academy, and studies reveal that it contains on average a mistake every ten lines, supporting the belief that it was copied in haste.

The Walk

If you drive a car to Lislahelly, please find an unobtrusive roadside space to park, or ask permission to park beside someone's house. If you use bus services along the main roads, then walk to Lislahelly, then the distance for the day will be around 24km (15 miles).

1. Start at Lislahelly, on a minor road between Drumcliffe and Glencar. A short, narrow road leaves the minor road at a bend, where there is an attractive rockery at the junction. Follow the short, narrow road to reach two gates, and go through the one on the right. Keep to the left side of a field, following a line of trees towards an old farmhouse. Turn left around the farmhouse, then walk straight towards King's Mountain. A long and narrow field rises towards the mountain, divided only by a tumbled wall. Cross a fence at the top of the field to set foot on the steeper slopes above, then look carefully for the start of a zig-zag path on the steep and grassy slope **(15mins)**.

2. The path helps to ease the gradient on the ascent, slicing across the slope then heading into a steep-sided valley on the face of King's Mountain. When the path starts zig-zagging up to the right, leave it and climb straight to the head of the valley. You'll find another narrow path to follow, then you should head off to the left up a shallow valley. You have to cross a fence and a small stream before you can walk up this valley.

Rising to the left is the highest summit on King's Mountain. It looks like a limestone peak above a heather moorland, and a short, steep climb leads to the top. The height is 462m (1,527ft) and views are opening up very well **(1hr)**.

3. Retrace steps a short way from the limestone peak onto the heather moorland, then look ahead so that you can pick an easy course around the edge of the mountain. Generally, you'll be heading north-west towards the steepest end of Benbulbin, but as there is no definite path you can choose any course that suits you best. It is possible to walk on fairly easy ground simply by staying

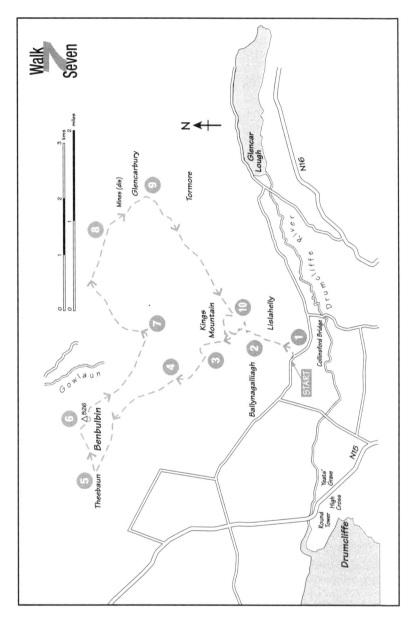

above the cliffs, but away from the rugged moorlands at a higher level. The vegetation cover is usually short, and some surfaces are stony. Cross a stream in a crumbling gully, then try and gain height gradually as you continue across a heather moorland slope **(1hr 15mins)**.

4. Cross a fence, then try and pick up a good sheep path across the slope, in order to avoid rougher areas of bog and heather. Cross another fence and climb a little higher to stay above the steep southern slopes of Benbulbin. The break of slope between the cliffs and moorland slopes becomes more prominent as you proceed. The end of the mountain is called Theebaun, where you should stop and admire the view **(2hrs)**.

    You might like to break for lunch here, with fine views along the low-lying coast and a great sense of depth while you're seated on the very prow of Benbulbin. The time allowance for the walk includes an hour for lunch at this point.

5. Turn all the way around the end of Benbulbin and follow the northern cliff-line. There are splendid gullies and buttresses in view, and in the summer months you'll see a variety of flowers decorating the rock, safe from grazing sheep. You can climb to the summit of Benbulbin by veering uphill away from the cliffs, crossing a grassy moorland to reach the trig point at 526m (1,730ft). It's worth pausing here to take in the view **(3hrs 15mins)**.

    Truskmore's broad shoulders and extra height obscure distant views to the east. You can let your eye rove from distant Cuilcagh and Slieve Anierin to the nearby Castlegal Range and Cope's Mountain. Slieve Daeane and the Bricklieve Mountains lie to the south, then the dome of Knocknarea and the long outline of the Ox Mountains lead the eye to Nephin and the Nephin Beg Range. Distant headlands include Downpatrick Head and Benwee Head. You can also see Slieve League, the Carrick Peninsula and the Blue Stack Mountains of Donegal.

6. Walk roughly south-east from the trig point on Benbulbin. You can choose to walk along the broad moorland crest, or follow the cliff line as you were before climbing to the summit. Any faint paths you find soon expire, then you cross a gentle rise of moorland. By keeping to the edge of the plateau, you can turn around the head of a valley, so that you then head more northwards. The limestone slope gives way to bog as you make the turn, then you walk on another limestone slope **(3hrs 45mins)**.

7. Walk along the break of slope near the edge of the plateau, and you'll be drawn more to the north-east, crossing a few little ups and downs along the way. When you reach another prominent valley, drift to the right and aim for its head. There are little swallow holes in the limestone, but also boggy patches. At the very head of the valley there is a stony gap with moorland to either side. This gap is at an altitude of 560m (1,835ft) and is the highest point gained on the walk **(4hrs 30mins)**.

8. Don't walk straight down into the valley beyond, but drift left

across the moorland slope to reach an area of mining spoil. A clear mining track leads downhill alongside a prominent deep cleft in the limestone. The track continues down to an electricity transmission line. A limestone knoll to the left is crowned with a small concrete cross, erected in Marian Year – 1954. You can climb to the cross, but retrace steps afterwards **(5hrs)**.

The mining area is known as Glencarbury, and there are chunks of a heavy, white mineral called barytes lying on the spoil heaps. Keep away from holes and clefts, which are liable to subsidence. You can also spot the pylons of an old aerial ropeway that was used to transport minerals down from the hills.

9. You can walk from Glencarbury to King's Mountain without gaining or losing too much height, but the slopes are pathless and quite rough in places. If you take a direct line, then first you cross a limestone area and ford a small stream. A rough stretch of bog and heather follows, then there is another limestone slope. Be careful, as the rock is broken and you could twist an ankle.

You can see the eastern summit of King's Mountain, but you should wander along the cliff edge to reach it, enjoying wonderful views of Glencar, its lake and surrounding hills. Keep to the edge of King's Mountain, where the ground bears stones and short heather. Amazing gullies and buttresses can be studied and there is a great sense of depth to the view. The summit on this side of King's Mountain rises to 436m (1,435ft), and so is slightly less than the other summit climbed earlier in the day's walk **(6hrs 15mins)**.

10. Descend from the cliff-line to reach a gap that is covered in stones, then turn left to follow a path downhill. There is a small stone cross perched above the path that marks the spot where two IRA volunteers were shot dead during the Civil War of 1922. Continue down the path, zig-zagging into the steep-sided valley that you climbed through earlier in the day. Simply retrace your steps downhill, walk back through the fields, turn right around the old farmhouse and walk back to the road **(7hrs)**.

Other walks in the area

Truskmore is the highest mountain in the area, and the only one with a road to its summit. Easy access is assured if you use the road to the tall transmitter mast, though there is plenty of wild country stretching eastwards towards Glenade away from the road.

Places of interest

The Drumcliffe Visitor Centre at the foot of Benbulbin offers plenty of information about the history and heritage of the area, from St. Columbkille to the poet Yeats. There is also the stump of a Round Tower and a fine sculptured high cross.

Walk 8:
Collooney, Slieve Daeane & Ballygawley
Strolling the Sligo Way

Slieve Daeane is a rugged little hill between Sligo city and the village of Collooney. The Sligo Way crosses the southern slopes of the hill using an old bog road between the summit and the lower forested slopes. You can enjoy a good day's walk by starting from Collooney, or shorten the route by starting from Ballygawley. Views from the high moorland slopes of Slieve Daeane stretch far across the low countryside to the south.

Grade: Moderate

Distance: 18km (11 miles)

Time: 6 hours (including an hour for lunch)

Start & Finish: Collooney Parish Church 680264

Map: Ordnance Survey of Ireland Discovery 25

How to get there
  By car: Collooney is just off the main N4 road south of Sligo city, near the junction with the main N5 heading west. Parking is available beside the road through the village.
  By bus: Bus Éireann table numbers 23, 64, 65, 76 & 461 all pass Collooney, but not every service allows a drop-off or pick-up, so please enquire beforehand. There are also Bus Éireann Imp services from Sligo city.
  By train: Collooney has an Iarnród Éireann station on the Dublin to Sligo line.

Necessities: Boots as the moorland slopes are wet and boggy; **walking shoes** are better for the roads; **waterproofs** as the moorland slopes are exposed in rain; **food and drink** for your lunch or; **money** for food and drink at Ballygawley.

Notes: The walk is well waymarked as part of the Sligo Way, and the roads used to close the circuit are easy and obvious to follow. You can either walk the full distance from Collooney, or enjoy a shorter walk by starting and finishing at Ballygawley.

Introduction

Collooney is easily spotted in many distant views simply by looking for the tall grey spire of its Parish Church. The village used to be something of a bottleneck on the main road south of Sligo, but it has been by-passed in recent years, leaving the streets quite empty of traffic. The main N4 road exploits a low gap between the Ox Mountains and Slieve Daeane, with the Dublin to Sligo railway running on a parallel course.

There are plenty of reminders of the 1798 Rebellion, commemorated in placenames in these parts. Just to the north of Collooney is the site of the Battle of Carrignagat. The English had stationed a cannon on Parkes Hill and this was preventing the French from advancing, until Bartholomew Teeling tore across country on his horse and shot the gunner dead. The name Teeling is highly regarded in the area and is even the name of the local sports centre. Camphill House is a place-name recalling how the French forces camped in the area. Union Rock commemorates a quite different event, only two years later in 1800, when the new Union Flag was flown after the passing of the Act of Union. Union Wood is mostly coniferous, but contains an ancient oakwood and a herd of fallow deer.

If you take a look at the map, you'll see the Dublin to Sligo railway running north to south through Collooney, but if you look more carefully you'll see two other disused railway lines; one heading east and the other heading west. In the brief heyday of the railways, Collooney was at the junction of the Waterford and Limerick Railway, the Midland and Great Western Railway, and the Sligo Leitrim and Northern Counties Railway.

The Sligo Way is followed away from Collooney, passing through Union Wood to reach Ballygawley Lough. After zig-zagging up a forested slope, the Sligo Way follows an old bog road across the southern slopes of Slieve Daeane and enjoys extensive views across the lowlands. There is a descent from Lough Lumman to a road near Lough Dargan, then there's a chance of a pub stop at Ballygawley on the way back to Collooney.

The Walk

Park somewhere convenient on the street in Collooney and you're ready to start walking. There are shops, pubs and restaurants if you need food or drink. The route follows the Sligo Way out of Collooney, so familiarise yourself with the signposts and marker posts.

1. To find the Sligo Way in Collooney, head for the prominent spire of the Parish Church. There is a shrine across the road and a Sligo Way signpost stands nearby. Walk down the road from the church, passing a school, then cross the old main road. Walk under a bridge on the new main road, following the broad Ballysadare River downstream. Turn left along a road marked as a cul de sac and cross a stone bridge. Turn left again along a narrow road and enter Union Wood at a fine gatehouse. There are curious stone pillars flanking the road **(30mins)**.

2. The tarmac gives way to a gravel forest road beside the river, then you turn right as indicated by a marker post, along another gravel track. Walk past a barrier, and the trees change from conifers to mossy oaks, with a fine understorey of holly, ivy and woodrush. Little cliffs are passed, then you turn right along another track. Walk uphill through coniferous forest again, then walk downhill

from a junction. Go straight through a point where track cross over, then keep right at another junction. After going through another crossing of tracks, rhododendron grows on either side of the track until you reach a gate onto a minor road near Ballygawley Lough (**1hr 30mins**).

3. Cross the road and walk uphill from a white house, passing through another gate. Walk straight up a slope that has been clear-felled of conifers, leaving isolated stands of beech and birch. Swing left as indicated by a marker post at a junction, then continue along the track to reach a turning space. Watch for markers to the

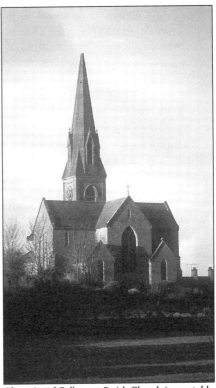

The spire of Collooney Parish Church is a notable landmark

right and left, as the paths and tracks you need to follow zig-zag across the higher forested slopes. Some parts are quite wet and muddy, and have been surfaced with plastic grids. Eventually you pass beneath powerlines and rise above the forest and follow a clear, but very wet and muddy track across the slopes of Slieve Daeane (**1hr 45mins**).

Note that Ordnance Survey maps are wrong in the way they depict Slieve Daeane. They show the forest rising all the way to the summit, but in fact the higher slopes have never been forested, nor are there any plans to plant trees on them.

4. Follow the clear track across the slopes of Slieve Daeane. There is plenty of rock, bog, squelchy sphagnum moss and heather, and the plastic grids in some places are a nuisance and are best avoided. Follow the direction indicated by the marker posts and you'll brush against one high part of the forest before crossing open slopes again. As the track swings gradually to the left, you'll reach an area where you can't see any habitations, though you're hardly in a remote area on this little hill. The track is quite wet and

muddy where it is lined with rhododendrons near Lough Lumman. At one point the Sligo Way touches the shore of the little moorland lough **(2hrs 30mins)**.

If you're looking for a pleasant spot to have your lunch, then sit beside Lough Lumman. The time allowance for the walk assumes you'll take an hour's break at this point. The rocks near the shore should be dry enough to sit on for lunch.

5. Follow the track onwards, downhill from Lough Lumman, to reach a metal Sligo Way signpost in an area of tree scrub. The Sligo Way turns left at this point, but you should continue your descent from Slieve Daeane by walking straight onwards on a muddy track. Straggly trees flank the track, as well as reeds and bog myrtle, as the ground really is very wet alongside. There are some rhododendrons, then you pass through an area of forest with some wide clearings, and continue downhill past a little house, a ruin and a farm to reach a minor road **(4hrs)**.

6. Turn right along the road, passing Lough Dargan, which is favoured by fishermen for its trout, pike and perch. Looking on the low horizon beyond the lough you can see the mouldering ruins of Castle Dargan. Follow the road until you reach a junction, where you turn left along the R284 road to reach Callaghan's Bar. There is a good view looking back to Slieve Daeane as you continue to the crossroads village of Ballygawley. Here you'll find Kelly's Bar and foodstore, as well as Ballygawley Post Office **(5hrs)**.

If you decide to take a break for a drink at either Callaghan's or Kelly's Bar, then be sure to allow extra time to complete the walk back to Collooney, especially if you are aiming to catch a particular bus or train. If you've deliberately chosen to walk all the way to Ballygawley before taking a lunch break, then you'll be more than ready for it!

7. Turn right to leave Ballygawley, as signposted for Collooney and the Tour de Humbert along the R290 road. Admire the distant view back to Slieve Daeane. You'll also see the green grassy ribbon of an old railway trackbed stretched across rushy fields parallel to the road. Cross an old stone bridge over the River Unshin, and note the fine old estate gateways **(5hrs 30mins)**.

8. You pass the entrance drive to the exclusive Markree Castle Hotel, then later pass a cemetery and the Teeling Sports Centre. Cross the main N4 road at a roundabout and walk back into Collooney. If you have the time you can retire to one of the pubs or the Teeling Restaurant for refreshments **(6hrs)**.

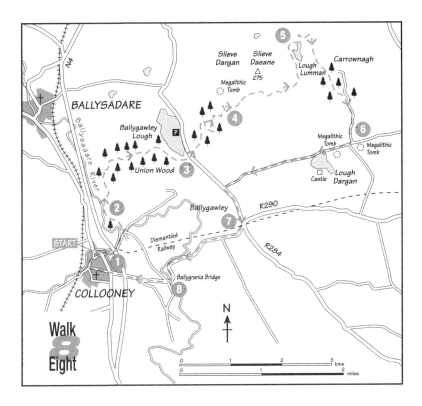

Other walks in the area

You could follow the course of the Sligo Way further eastwards to reach the shores of Lough Gill, or westwards towards the Ox Mountains. Obtain a copy of the Sligo Way Map Guide locally for details of the waymarked trail.

Places of interest

Sligo city has an interesting museum with a good section on the poet W. B. Yeats, as well as paintings by J. B. Yeats. The ruins of Sligo Abbey date from the 13th century and contains some fine stone carvings.

Walk 9:
Foxford & Carraighabhainn
Following the Foxford Way

Foxford is a fine little place clustered around a working woollen mill on the banks of the salmon-rich River Moy. The Foxford Way leaves the mills and wanders in a wide loop through the surrounding countryside, as well as having a spur through the rugged Ox Mountains. If you start following the Foxford Way, you can cross a rugged little hill at Roosky and descend to Carraighabhainn. There is an interesting Open Farm where you could break for refreshments, then follow quiet roads back to Foxford.

Grade: Moderate

Distance: 17km (10½ miles)

Time: 5½ hours (including an hour for lunch)

Start & Finish: Foxford Woollen Mills 270043

Map: Ordnance Survey of Ireland Discovery 31

How to get there

By car: Foxford is on the main N26 road between Swinford and Ballina. It can also be approached from Bellavary and Straide using the N58 road, or from Castlebar and Pontoon using the R310 and R318 roads. There is a car park beside the Foxford Woollen Mills, and you'll find the mills are well signposted from all the approach roads.

By bus: Bus Éireann table number 22 offers a daily service to Foxford from Dublin and Ballina. Table numbers 66 & 69 links Foxford with Westport, Castlebar, Ballina and Sligo.

By Train: Foxford has an Iarnród Éireann station on the railway line from Dublin to Ballina.

Necessities: Boots as the higher parts are boggy though **walking shoes** will do for the lower ground; **waterproofs** as there is no shelter on the high ground; **money** to visit the Open Farm and to buy **food and drink** there.

Notes: For the most part, this is a pleasant and easy walk along quiet roads and tracks. However, there is a rugged, boggy hill to be crossed and care is needed with navigation in mist. You could walk round the hill by road, through Glandaduff, if you wanted an easy walk without crossing the hill. When the Carraigabhainn Open Farm is open to visitors, you can have a look around and break for refreshments.

Introduction

Foxford has an intriguing claim to fame. The founder of the Argentine Navy, Admiral William Brown, was born and reared in the village. His family emigrated to America and William became a cabin boy on an American merchant vessel. He later joined the Royal Navy and was captured by the French during the Napoleonic Wars. After effecting an escape and returning to England, he married and travelled to Buenos Aires. When one of his vessels was attacked by the Spanish, he not only became involved in a rebellion against Spanish domination, but helped to establish the Argentine Navy and secured a victory over the Spanish. He returned briefly to Ireland in the aftermath of the Great Famine, and found it distressing, so returned to Buenos Aires to live out his days.

The story of the Foxford Woollen Mills is the subject of a walk-though multi-media presentation, and one that is highly recommended. It was all very different at the start, when Mother Agnes Morrogh Bernard of the Sisters of Charity visited Foxford and was appalled at the level of poverty in the area some years after the Great Famine. The only produce in the area was corn, and the corn mill beside the River Moy was derelict. Mother Agnes founded the Providence Mills in 1892, and along with it a comprehensive system of education, building and improvement. When the Sisters of Charity finally ceased their involvement in the enterprise, it continued both as a woollen mills and a visitor attraction. Woollens are on sale in the mills, as well as other crafts, and there is a fine restaurant on site too.

The Foxford Way has been steered and waymarked through the countryside and the wide loop is seldom far removed from Foxford. There is a rugged spur through the Ox Mountains which would suit hillwalkers, but much of the course is along quiet roads and tracks through gentle countryside. A fine sample of the route can be enjoyed from the Foxford Woollen Mills to the Carraigabhainn Open Farm, returning along minor roads. If you're counting on refreshments being available at the Open Farm, check in advance by phoning 094-56444. It is usually open every afternoon, but is closed on Saturdays.

The Walk

There is a car park beside the Foxford Woollen Mills at the start of the Foxford Way. If the Visitor Centre is open, then you might like to spend an hour there before starting the walk, otherwise check the times of last admission and explore it later in the day.

1. Follow the narrow road away from the Foxford Woollen Mills, downstream alongside the broad River Moy. You pass a big house and a nursing home, as well as a couple of sports pitches. There is a view of the domed mountain called Nephin far away across the river, and you'll see it from many other parts of the walk too. At the end of the tarmac road, turn right along a gravel track, crossing level fields divided by fences. You can see the day's hill ahead of you, and you'll become accustomed to the waymark posts that indicate your route. Turn left along a minor road **(30mins)**.

2. Follow the road, then turn left at the next junction, followed by a right turn. The road crosses the Yellow River and reaches another junction with a wider road. Turn left here, then look out for a track leading off to the right **(1hr)**.

3. The track follows an undulating course, gradually rising and passing patchy woodlands and small fields. Mossy boulders flank the

track and one part is quite close to the edge of a gravel pit. There are old houses and small farms along the way. Turn right along a narrow, battered old road that has a grassy strip along the middle for much of its length. Turn right up another road at Roosky, leading up into a rugged valley. The scene looks almost mountainous, but in fact you're at no great height. Turn right at a three-fingered signpost for the Foxford Way **(1hr 45mins)**.

(If the weather is wet and miserable, you might prefer to omit the hill walk over Roosky Mountain, in which case you can follow the road further uphill from Roosky to Glandaduff. You can then turn right and follow another road to the Carraighabhainn Open Farm on the far side of the hill.)

4. Leaving the road, a stony track rises up through a shallow, rugged valley and there are fine views looking back downhill. The track expires at a series of turf cuttings and you need to refer more carefully to your map. In mist, you should be ready to use your compass too **(2hrs)**.

5. The course of the Foxford Way is basically south-east across the rugged Roosky Mountain, but the markers lead you around rocky and boggy areas, and so there are a series of turns to the left and right. You need to look ahead to spot the markers, walking across wet and boggy areas, up and down heathery slopes, avoiding little outcrops of rock along the way. The highest parts of Roosky Mountain rise only to 270m (885ft), and although the hill is only small, it can be confusing if you lose the line of markers in mist.

    Look out for feral goats as you cross the hill. Goats are quite common in the Ox Mountains and although they look wild, they are actually descended from farm stock. There is an annual Goat Fair in Foxford on 15th May. It is based on an original patent for a market fair which dates from 1683.

6. When you link with a grassy track on the far side of the hill, simply turn right and follow it downhill. There is a quick turn left and right further downhill so that you can follow another track between low drystone walls. This track is choked with heather and gorse in places, but otherwise leads straight down to a gate and a minor road. When you reach the road you can either turn left for the Carraigabhainn Open Farm, or right to return directly to Foxford **(3hrs)**.

    The Carraigabhainn Open Farm is generally open in the afternoon, but not on Saturday. It is a working farm run on traditional lines, with livestock such as cows and sheep, along with Tamworth pigs, deer, goats, donkey and poultry. Trees have been planted and wild flowers are encouraged in all sorts of corners. There are sometimes demonstrations of traditional skills, including a 'fulachta fia', showing how Bronze Age people cooked venison in water-filled pits using stones heated in a fire alongside to boil the water.

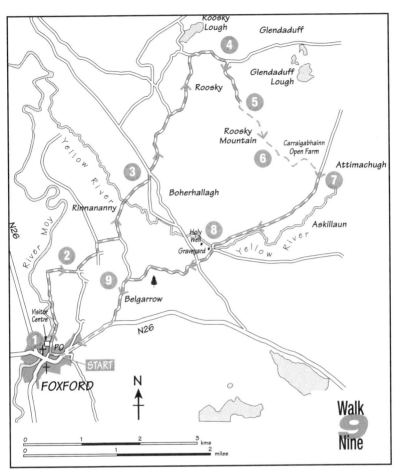

There is a tea room in an old granary where you can also sample home produce. In fact, Carraigabhainn is ideally situated for a lunch break, and the time allowance for the walk includes an hour spent on site. If you stay any longer, you should allow for that when calculating the time needed to return to Foxford afterwards.

7. When you leave Carraigabhainn, turn right to follow the narrow minor road through the valley drained by the Yellow River. You'll notice that the Foxford Way heads off to the left, down to the river, but you should keep following the road instead. After passing a few farms and houses, the road crosses a bridge over the Yellow River **(4 hrs 30mins)**.

    Notice the old graveyard above the Yellow River, just to the right of the road. Any stones with inscriptions are relatively recent, but there are plenty of rough, uninscribed stones that mark older graves. The level of the graveyard is substantially higher than the land immediately alongside, suggesting that it is quite an ancient plot.

8. Turn right along another minor road and go straight through a crossroads later. The road passes a gravel pit, then runs alongside a wild and wooded area. There is another graveyard, this time a modern one, and another gravel pit. Turn left at the next road junction **(5hrs)**.

    The gravel pits in the area are working thick deposits of glacial moraine, sifting and sorting the rubble into different sizes for different applications in the construction industry.

9. Follow the minor road to a junction with the main N26 road. Just across the road is a bouldery grotto to Our Lady of Lourdes. Turn right to follow the main road straight towards Foxford. When you enter the village, you can turn right along a quiet road at the Post Office to return directly to the Foxford Woollen Mills, or follow the main road into the centre of the village where there are a few shops and pubs **(5hrs 30mins)**.

Other walks in the area

The Foxford Way offers the chance to enjoy low-level walks in a farming landscape, as well as a high-level route through the Ox Mountains. Obtain a copy of the Foxford Way guidebook locally to help you choose a good section to walk.

Places of interest

Apart from the Foxford Woollen Mills and the Carraigabhainn Open Farm visited on this walk, you can also visit Hennigan's Farm Heritage Centre and the Davitt Museum at Straide, with the ruins of Straide Abbey alongside.

Carraigabhainn Open Farm is well worth a visit

Walk 7: Looking down into the deeply-cut barytes mine

Walk 9: Walkers follow a rugged track from Rooskey to Rooskey Mountain

Walk 10: A rigged pinnacle of rock seen at the base of the cliffs

Walk 14: Ireland's National Famine Monument at the foot of Croagh Patrick

Walk 12: Looking down on Lough Nakeeroge on Achill Island

Walk 19: A view of the Twelve Bens from near the old limekiln

Walk 20: Mist creeps across the shoulder of Benbaun as seen from Benfree

Walk 10:
Portacloy Benwee Head & Carrowteige
Cliffs and coves

Benwee Head is one of those significant turning points on the Irish coastline. While much of the Connacht coast features a barrage of islands between the broad Atlantic and the mainland, there's nothing to protect Benwee Head from the full force and fury of the ocean. It is an exposed headland, whose cliffs are battered and broken, and in a remote part of the country, served only by empty roads leading to the tiny little villages of Portacloy and Carrowteige.

Grade: Moderate

Distance: 20km (12½ miles)

Time: 7 hours (including an hour for lunch)

Start & Finish: At the bridge near the beach at Portacloy 840440

Maps: Ordnance Survey of Ireland Discovery 22 & 23

How to get there

By car: The R314 road runs in a loop around the North Mayo Coast between Ballina, Ballycastle and Belmullet. When you follow this road, turn off it at the tiny settlement of Glenamoy and follow an empty minor road across a broad bogland. There are turnings for Rossport and Porturlin, but you should keep straight on to reach the turning for Carrowteige and Portacloy. Turn right for Portacloy.

By bus: This area is well off the usual bus routes. A local daily minibus service is operated by McGrath's Coaches, linking Portacloy and Carrowteige with Ballina and Castlebar. Phone 097-88915 for details.

Necessities: Stout shoes should suffice instead of boots; **waterproofs** as the cliffs are exposed in wet weather; **food and drink** as there's nothing until you reach the shop at Carrowteige; **money** for a drink at Connolley's Bar if you're prepared to make a slight detour.

Notes: The walk around Benwee Head is an exceptionally good cliff walk. On a fine day you can marvel at the colours of the rock and enjoy distant views. On a windy day you can watch the breakers pounding the foot of the cliffs and striking the rocky stacks. The latter half of the walk is altogether quieter, linking tracks and roads through Carrowteige to return to Portacloy.

Introduction

During the dark years of the Great Famine, Richard Webb toured this part of Connacht and reported back to the Society of Friends. He was dismayed at what he found around Portacloy and Porturlin, concluding that there was no easy access either by land or sea. Between 1846 and 1910, work was slowly completed so that roads crossed the bogs, bridges were built over the rivers, and piers were built at the villages.

Even today, however, many people who follow the road across the bog wonder where on earth it is leading them!

Facilities around Benwee Head are very limited. If you have no car, then please take note of the fact that McGrath's Coaches can bring you in from towns as distant as Castlebar and Ballina. There is only one farmhouse B&B, which is Stag View, perched high above the sandy bay at Portacloy. There is a shop in the nearby settlement of Carrowteige, and a bar at Stonefield. If you want one of the best coastal walks in Ireland, then despite the dearth of facilities, you're in the right place.

The walk around Benwee Head has some steep and rugged slopes in places, but on the whole it is a fairly straightforward walk. Some parts are covered in such delightfully short grass that you'd almost be inclined to walk it barefoot. There is a striking headland near the start that bears the remains of a promontory fort, and the site remains as difficult to approach today as it did when it was built. Rock stacks and a small island look particularly vulnerable out in the ocean, and the cliffs are well and truly battered by the elements. There is so little vegetation on some of them that it's quite easy to see the underlying geology and pick out every layer of rock and some amazing patterns of folding.

It is worth taking your time on this walk, even to the extent of spending a weekend or more getting to know the place better. It is a 'Gaeltacht', or Irish speaking area, and in the summer months boys and girls are quartered among the local population to learn the language.

The Walk

When you finally reach the end of the road at Portacloy Bay, you're almost on the sandy beach. You'll find a place to park near the bridge over the river, quite close to the beach.

1. Leave the bridge over the river at the head of Portacloy Bay and follow the road uphill. You pass above two concrete piers to reach the end of the road, then continue through a small gate in a fence. Cross a stream and follow a vague path across a slope of short grass and heather. This leads to a small concrete hut on a rugged point. There are fine views along the cliffs and out to the Stags of Broadhaven **(20mins)**.

2. Retrace your steps a short way, spotting the word 'EIRE' laid out in huge stone letters.

    'EIRE' was marked at intervals around the north-west coast of Ireland in the Second World War, warning aircraft pilots not to land in neutral Ireland. Even those who landed in an emergency, or survived a crash-landing, were liable to be interned.

You may not believe in leprechauns and pots of gold, but there's a little hollow full of coins you might spot if you keep your eyes open!

Climb uphill to the right, and as you turn around the top of a rock-walled cove, look at the outstanding headland that features the remains of a promontory fort. It looks as though it could be reached only by rock-climbers, and its situation was obviously ideal. Looking inland, Portacloy is revealed as a scattered settlement of farms and houses in a green valley surrounded by hills and bog **(30mins)**.

Looking back at chaotic stacks, cliffs and headlands

3. The next rocky bay displays sloping cliffs cut into sharp, angular forms that are really quite remarkable. Short lengths of post and wire fencing keep you away from crumbling cliff edges. When you look back later, you'll see pronounced zig-zag folding in the cliffs, as well as several caves along the base. A double-spiked jagged rock protruding from the rocky cove is a notable feature as you climb onto the next grassy hill. Walk downhill and cross a gap that can be wet, and look down to the pyramidal stacks and the jagged headland pierced with a hole. A fence keeps you away from the cliff edge on the highest part of Benwee Head at 255m (829ft). The summit is covered in blanket bog **(1hr 30mins)**.

4. Looking along the cliff-line, you'll notice that the sea is filled with rock stacks, and in the distance is the gentle green crest of Kid Island. Simply follow the cliff line onwards, walking out onto the headlands and turning round the rocky coves in between. After walking round the first headland and cove, you reach a road-end, which is useful if you need to divert inland early **(2hrs)**.

5. A turf bank runs roughly parallel to the cliffs and the walk appears to be heading towards a grassy hill. In fact, the hill turns out to be Kid Island, and a rugged little strait full of stacks opens up as you reach the headland **(2hrs 30mins)**.

    This is a fine place to sit down and have lunch, though in wild and wet weather you might prefer to keep moving. The time allowance for the walk includes an hour for lunch overlooking Kid Island.

6. As you turn around the headland, the turf bank leads straight onwards and you might as well continue following its course. You could walk on the seaward side of the bank and explore a handful of little headlands, but the walk becomes more of a roller-coaster if you do that. You cross a steep-sided little river valley, then follow the turf bank straight uphill. At the top, bear right and walk out onto a final rugged headland, then turn left around its end **(4hrs 30mins)**.

7. Continue along a lower cliff-line overlooking Broad Haven. At one point a fence squeezes you rather close to the cliff edge, but if you enter the field it encloses you can proceed by using little gates further uphill. A sandy, grassy slope leads down to a lovely, sandy bay and a narrow tarmac road. The road runs out onto Rinroe Point, but if you follow it you have to retrace your steps afterwards **(5hrs)**.

8. Cross over the road, then follow a track across a sandy, grassy expanse to reach a prominent graveyard at the foot of a hill. Looking uphill, you'll see a small settlement known as Stonefield. There is an ancient cairn in the graveyard as well as a more modern Marian shrine. Follow a narrow, fenced, tarmac road uphill and keep rising gently past a junction. The road is flanked by trees and bushes in places, which makes quite a change after the treeless cliff walking. There are a few houses, and at the top of the road you turn right to pass through the settlement of Carrowteige **(5hrs 45mins)**.

    At Carrowteige you could turn left to reach Connolley's Bar at Stonefield, but if you turn right to continue with the walk, then you'll pass a telephone box, small knitwear factory and a shop.

9. Follow the road downhill from Carrowteige and it runs out across a broad bogland. Walk straight through a road junction at the bottom and you'll be led back to the head of Portacloy Bay **(7hrs)**.

Other walks in the area

The local community in this sparsely settled area have produced a booklet called Dun Caochain Walks, which covers the wonderful cliff coastline and broad boglands between Belderrig and Carrowteige.

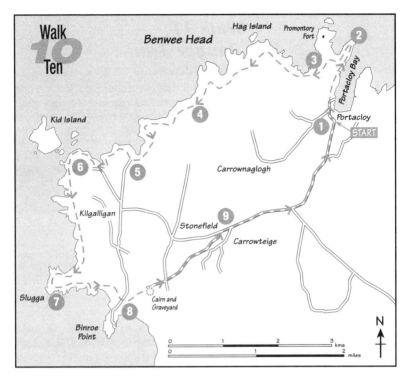

Walk
10
Ten

Benwee Head

Hag Island   Promontory
Fort

Portacloy Bay

Portacloy

START

Kid Island

Carrownaglogh

Kilgalligan

Stonefield

Carrowteige

Slugga

Binroe
Point

Cairn and
Graveyard

N

0   1   2   3 kms
0   1   2 miles

Places of interest

In this area, most people head for the Ceide Fields Visitor Centre, perched on the cliffs between Ballycastle and Belderrig, where ancient field boundaries have been discovered buried beneath 5,000 years of accumulated bog. There is also the interesting Tir Saile Sculpture Trail signposted all around the north coast of Mayo.

Walk 11:
The Bangor Trail
Droving and roving

The Bangor Trail has been around for two centuries; possibly much longer. The old drove road linked Newport and Bangor Erris and has been waymarked for walkers. As the early stages are along roads, you might as well concentrate on the stretch from Srahmore Lodge to Bangor Erris. The trail crosses the bleak and barren Nephin Beg Range and skirts the edge of an awesome tract of broad blanket bog. Although there are plentiful signs of engineering along the way, the trail has been overwhelmed by bog in places and is quite rugged in other parts. There are no easy escape routes, and only one basic shelter.

Grade: Strenuous

Distance: 26km (16 miles)

Time: 9 hours (including an hour for lunch)

Start: Srahmore Lodge north of Newport 974045.

Finish: Bangor Erris 863232.

Map: Ordnance Survey of Ireland Discovery 23.

How to get there

> *By car:* Leave Newport following the N59 towards Mulranny. Turn right along a minor road for Traenlaur Youth Hostel, beside Lough Feeagh. Continue along the road beyond the hostel to reach Srahmore Lodge, or maybe continue along the rough road a little further to shorten the route a little. If someone can drive back from Srahmore, and follow the N59 to Mulranny and Bangor Erris, then they can wait for you at the far end.
>
> *By bus:* Bus Éireann table numbers 66, 69, 440 & 441 serve Newport. You'll have to walk to Srahmore Lodge. Table number 446 serves Bangor Erris. The only way to connect these services is via the distant towns of Castlebar and Ballina.

Necessities: Boots as the trail is rough, wet and boggy; **waterproofs** as there is virtually no cover from the rain and wind; **torch** in case you run out of daylight; **plenty of food and drink** in case you spend the night out; **money** for food, drink and accommodation at Bangor Erris when you get there; **the weather forecast** should be a good one!

Notes: Make no mistake, this is a rough, tough walk. When the weather is foul, leave it well alone and make another choice. Don't be misled by the low-level nature of the route, as it crosses bleak mountain slopes remote from habitation. On a clear day, however, with plenty of time and energy on your side, the trail offers a taste of the wilderness and amazingly extensive views.

Introduction

The Bangor Trail is the best way to sample the broad boglands and wilderness around the Nephin Beg Range. Pick a clear day to complete this walk, and be sure to allow plenty of time, starting early in the

Pausing to admire the view on a remote part of the Bangor Trail

morning and keeping a careful note of your progress as the hours of daylight trickle away. It is useful if someone can drop you at Srahmore Lodge and wait for you at Bangor Erris, otherwise you'll have difficulty trying to fit the walk in between the available bus services.

Many walkers find the Bangor Trail difficult underfoot. Although the trail was engineered through the wilderness, it hasn't been maintained for well over a century and the bog has made great advances on it. Expect the trail itself to be rocky or boggy, sometimes to the extent that it is easier to walk alongside it. Posts bearing green waymark arrows and numbers mark the route. Selected numbered posts are mentioned in this route description. There are no easy escapes from the route, and the only shelter is a tiny hut in the middle that was flown in by helicopter. Bear the existence of this shelter in mind, but don't set out with the intention of staying there overnight, as it really is only an emergency provision. Given that the route is quite difficult, you might prefer to stay overnight at Bangor Erris when you get there, rather than trying to travel anywhere else. If you choose this option, book your accommodation in advance.

There is an annual walk along the Bangor Trail, traditionally held on the Saturday closest to Midsummer's Day, in order to make the most use of the long daylight hours. Numbers are limited to one hundred, so that there isn't an adverse impact on the terrain. There is 'free' beer, included in the entry fee levied on the day, and organised transport, to save you the bother of organising a pick-up. For those who can still stand upright, the event ends with everyone dancing through the night!

The Walk

You can drive your car from Newport, past Traenlaur Lodge Youth Hostel, to Srahmore Lodge. You can go a short way beyond the lodge, but watch for the waymarks pointing left for the Bangor Trail and Western Way, just as you cross a river. The Bangor Trail marker post is number 13 in the series from Newport. If you plan to do the 'two car trick' and leave one car here, there is a forest car park further along where you can leave it without causing an obstruction.

1. At first, the Bangor Trail, waymarked by green arrows, runs con-current with the Western Way, marked by yellow arrows. A level walk through the forest leads from the Srahrevagh River to the Altaconey River. The Western Way heads off to the right, but the Bangor Trail turns left at waymark 14 and crosses a wooden foot-bridge over the Altaconey River. **(15 minutes)**

    The footbridge was constructed specially for walkers on the Bangor Trail. It was built during a hot and humid spell and the workers named it 'The Bridge over the River Kwai' on account of their trouble with biting midges! It is worth bearing in mind that the broad boglands and stagnant pools around the Nephin Beg Range are ideally suited for breeding midges. The problem is that there are very few animals for adult female midges to draw blood from... that is... until you appear on the scene!

2. The Bangor Trail runs upstream beside another river, but there is no footbridge and you have to cross using boulders as stepping stones. If this river proves difficult to cross in wet weather, and yet is passable, you can be assured that there are no more difficult fords between here and Bangor Erris **(30mins)**.

3. The Bangor Trail runs uphill alongside Letterkeen Wood, crossing the shoulder of a hill at 200m (650ft). A short descent takes the trail alongside another part of Letterkeen Wood, then it runs alongside the Bawnduff River, through a significant gap in the Nephin Beg Range **(1hr 15mins)**.

    You begin to appreciate the remoteness of the surroundings as you struggle along the rugged trail, crossing a number of small streams. The ruins of an old farm are passed, close to an oak tree which is one of the few trees you'll see on this route. The trail climbs up a rugged slope to reach a shoulder of Nephin Beg at 260m (850ft). This is the highest point on the Bangor Trail and you can be sure of your position as waymark number 20 stands here. Views stretch across a broad and boggy moorland hollow at Scardaun **(2hrs)**.

    You are about a third of the way along the trail, but the further you proceed, the more you have to commit yourself to reaching Bangor Erris. If the time or weather is against you at this point, then please turn back to Srahmore Lodge.

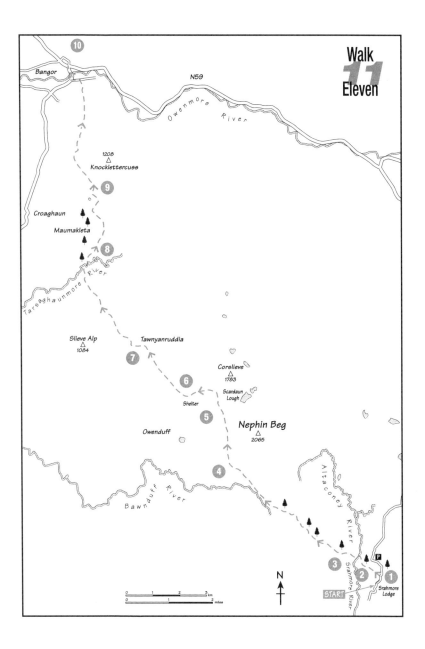

4. To continue with the walk, follow the trail downhill across the rugged slopes of Nephin Beg. At waymark number 21 **(2hrs 30 minutes)** there is a track heading off to the left that leads to Srahduggan, but it is too long to be considered as a good escape route.

5. Keep walking and cross over a stream that tumbles downhill as a waterfall from Scardaun Lough; the lough itself being out of sight in a gap between Nephin Beg and Corslieve. The trail swings around a huge hollow in the hills and reaches a small hut at Owenduff **(3hrs)**.

   The hut was flown in by helicopter and dropped into the ruins of an old building as an emergency shelter. If you find you are running out of energy, running out of time, or experiencing foul weather, then this is the only shelter available on the whole of the Bangor Trail. A night spent in the hut would be only marginally better than a bivouac on the open mountainside. You have been warned! If you stop here for lunch, the time given at the start of this description includes a break of one hour.

6. Leaving Owenduff you may consider yourself embarking on the second half of the trail, but it is disheartening to realise that the ground conditions are no easier. The trail contours around the rugged slopes of Tawnyanruddia and climbs onto the shoulder of the mountain. Waymark number 24 stands on this shoulder and views are quite extensive **(4hrs 45mins)**.

   You can look roughly northwards in the direction of Bangor Erris, but because of the topography you can't actually see the village. The broad slopes of the Nephin Beg Range limits the prospects north, east and south, but there is a grand and extensive view to the west. It takes a while to realise that most of the big, brown hills and mountains in view are actually on Achill Island. These include Knockmore, the Minaun Heights, Slievemore and Croaghaun. You can also see Belmullet and the distant Benwee Head. Enjoy the view, but please keep an eye on your progress.

7. The trail descends from the shoulder of the mountain and follows a river downstream. Don't walk too close to the river, but stay on the brow of the little valley through which it runs. You have to ford a couple of tributary streams, but these shouldn't cause too much difficulty even in wet weather.

   Looking ahead, and a little to the right, you should be able to see a footbridge spanning the Tarsaghaunmore River, and you can walk straight towards it. The bridge is long and narrow, and was constructed specially for walkers on the trail, and this is just as well, as the river is a sight to behold when swollen with brown bog water after heavy rain **(6hrs 15mins)**.

   If you need an escape route at this point, you could walk downstream and follow a farm access road to the main N59 road. At that point, you could either turn right to follow the main road to Bangor Erris, or try to hitch a lift there. In terms of distance, there's little between this option and the main route, but it is the only way you can bail out easily.

8. Follow the trail uphill from the footbridge, slicing across the slopes of a hill called Mamakleta. The route misses the summits of Mamakleta and neighbouring Croaghaun Mountain, passing through a boggy gap between Croaghaun Mountain and Knocklettercuss. The height of the gap is almost 220m (720ft) and at last you can look ahead to spot Bangor Erris **(7hrs 30mins)**.

9. The Bangor Trail descends from the gap and crosses the head of the boggy hollow called Muingnahallona. Although in its closing stages, the surface of the trail remains wet and rugged. The gradient is gentler as the route cuts across the slopes of Knocklettercuss, then there is a final descent towards a playing field **(8hrs 45mins)**.

10. The first firm, dry footing is gained since leaving Srahmore Lodge. Simply turn left and follow the minor road from the playing field to the main N59 road, then turn right to cross the Owenmore River. This is a notable salmon river; expect it to be busy with fishermen in the summer. The road leads straight to a crossroads in the middle of Bangor Erris **(9hrs)**.

   There is a small range of accommodation in Bangor Erris, if you decide to stay overnight, and there is food and drink available in bars along the main street. If you plan to leave by bus, then you will doubtless need to stay overnight and catch the bus in the morning. Using bus services to return to Newport via Ballina and Castlebar could take all day, if you had to return to Srahmore Lodge to retrieve your car.

Other walks in the area

You could extend this walk by including the waymarked stretch of the Bangor Trail along roads and tracks from Newport to Srahmore Lodge. Obtain a copy of the Bangor Trail guidebook locally for details. You can use the trail to reach the higher parts of the Nephin Beg Range, bearing in mind that these are broad, bleak mountains.

Places of interest

Newport is an interesting little town, and its old railway bridge and Parish Church are beautifully floodlit at night.

Walk 12:
Dooagh, Croaghaun & Achill Head
Scrambling by the sea

Achill Island is the largest Irish island, but as you cross the short causeway across the narrow Achill Sound, you'll hardly realise you're leaving the mainland and reaching an island. Achill is covered in some of the deepest blanket bogs in Ireland, but you'll also find some of the tallest sea cliffs in Europe. The walk over Croaghaun allows you to marvel at these cliffs, and if you're feeling fit and agile, then you could scramble out onto Achill Head, whose bony finger points west into the broad and empty Atlantic Ocean. Choose a fine day for the walk, both for safety's sake and to enjoy the extensive views.

Grade: Moderate to strenuous

Distance: 26km (16 miles)

Time: 8 hours (including an hour for lunch)

Start & Finish: At the village of Dooagh on Achill Island 605049

Map: Ordnance Survey of Ireland Discovery 30

How to get there
> *By car:* The usual approach to Achill Island is from Westport and Newport, following the N59 road to Mulranny. At this point, switch to the R319 road signposted for Achill. The road runs round the Corraun peninsula, then crosses a causeway to reach Achill Sound. Simply continue along the road through Cashel and Keel to reach the village of Dooagh.
> *By bus:* Bus Éireann table numbers 66, 69, 440 & 441 serve Dooagh. If you study the full timetables, you'll see that table numbers 66 & 69 connect with services as far away as Enniskillen and Belfast.

Necessities: Boots as the slopes are rough and steep; **waterproofs** as there is virtually no cover from the rain and wind; **food and drink** to keep up the energy levels; **money** for food and drink at Dooagh; **the weather forecast** should be good for the sake of the views.

Notes: This is a walk to savour in fine weather. Mist deprives you of the most astounding views, and rain can make some of the steep slopes of short grass treacherously slippery. Check the weather forecast. It is also important to take care near the cliff edges, especially on Croaghaun, where large cracks are gradually opening and a tremendous rockfall is surely imminent.

Introduction

Achill Island is so close to the mainland that you wouldn't immediately notice the narrow channel that separates the two landmasses. The causeway to the island was equipped with a swing bridge, but this is never opened, so the island is permanently connected to the mainland. In the height of summer, and especially on fine weekends, the is-

Bunnatreva Lough West fills a coum high on Croaghaun

land can become quite crowded and all the accommodation can be fully booked, but at other times of the year you should be able to secure lodgings.

Walking on Achill always brings excellent views of the sea, and there are so many hills and cliffs to explore. The huge, heathery pudding of Slievemore dominates most views, but Croaghaun is a little higher and certainly has more extensive cliffs. While Achill Head's cliffs have to be approached on foot to be appreciated, you could almost drive to the top of the Minaun Heights to have a look at the Minaun Cliffs. This is highly recommended when there is a fiery sunset, as the colours are truly amazing, but if you do that, then please take a torch so that you don't run into difficulties at nightfall.

There is an interesting feature you'll notice soon after starting the walk, off-route on the flanks of Slievemore. The gaunt, grey ruins of a deserted village lie alongside an old road. This is an atmospheric place and is well worth a visit. You'll also pass a ruined signal tower that was once part of a series of towers built to keep an eye on shipping. There is a more recent lookout tower towards the end of the walk on Moyteoge Head, as well as a reminder of Ireland's neutrality in the Second World War, when you spot the word 'EIRE' marked out in stone for the benefit of passing warplanes.

There is a cottage on the way back to Dooagh where you can buy chunks of local amethyst. You should also look out for a commemorative stone recording the arrival of Don Allum; the only man ever to have rowed both ways across the Atlantic Ocean. The pub across the road has photographs and information about the event.

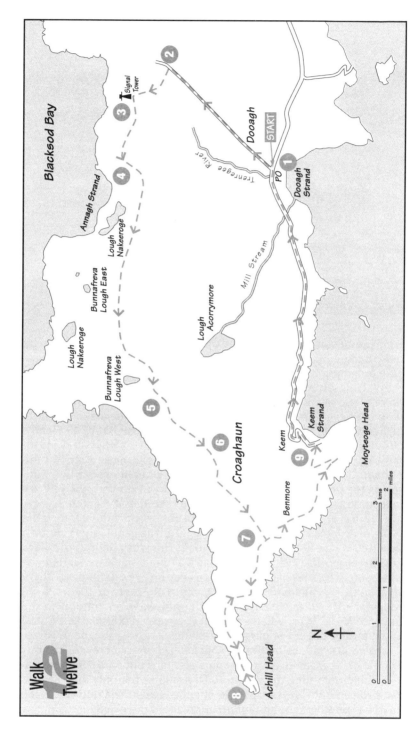

Walk
Twelve

Blacksod Bay

② ④

③ Signal
Tower

Dooagh

START

Annagh Strand

PO

Dooagh
Strand

Trenragee River

Lough
Nakeeroge

Lough
Nakeeroge

Bunnafreva
Lough East

Mill Stream

Lough
Acorrymore

Bunnafreva
Lough West

⑤

⑥

Croaghaun

Keem

Keem
Strand

⑨

Benmore

Moyteoge Head

⑦

N

Achill Head

⑧

The Walk

The drive across Achill Island passes a multitude of whitewashed houses scattered at random across the fields and hillsides. When you reach Dooagh, you can park overlooking Dooagh Strand. This is also the terminus for Bus Éireann services to and from the island.

1. Whether you park overlooking Dooagh Strand, or arrive by bus, start walking near the Post Office and follow a minor road inland to pass the Atlantic Hotel. The tarmac gives way to a pebbly track that rises gently uphill, passing a few little fields and more extensive areas of turf cuttings. When you reach the crest of the track, the huge dome of Slievemore rises ahead and you can pick out the ruins of a deserted village on its lower slopes (**45mins**).

2. Turn left to walk away from the top of the track, crossing a small area of turf cuttings before climbing up a small, heathery hill. The summit rises to 194m (645ft) and is crowned with the ruins of an old signal tower (**1hr**).

    The situation was ideal for the signal tower, as the hill is generally below the cloudbase, yet is high enough to be seen easily from adjacent signal towers on the Belmullet Peninsula and Clare Island.

3. Walk due west and cross a gentle gap in the hills. A short climb leads up a heathery slope to another rounded summit at 269m (891ft). The covering of blanket bog has gone, revealing the shiny schist bedrock beneath (**1hr 15mins**).

    Enjoy the view of Lough Nakeeroge; a long and narrow pool of water suspended just above Annagh Strand. Prepare yourself for splendid scenery as the walk progresses.

4. Walk south-west for a short while to avoid outcrops of rock on the side of the hill, then cross another gentle gap and another rounded summit. Heather cover gives way to grass on the way down to a broad and boggy gap overlooking Lough Nakeeroge. Climb up a steep heathery slope, which is quite bouldery at first. At a higher level the gradient eases and you walk more gently uphill along a broad, grassy, boggy shoulder. Pools of water are passed, then the ground is rather stony. Swing to the left around a steep, rocky edge, where there are splendid views into the deep coum holding Bunnatreva Lough West (**2hrs 45mins**).

5. After walking round the head of the coum, you reach the steep and rugged cliffs that tumble chaotically from Croaghaun to the Atlantic Ocean. Follow the edge onwards, but please keep well back as there are some awesome cracks and fissures, and masses of fractured rock are bound to go crashing down to the sea sooner or later. One final steep, heathery, boulder-strewn slope needs to be climbed to reach the summit cairn on Croaghaun at 688m

(2,260ft). From this vantage point, you notice that the sea is wrapped around three sides of the view **(3hrs 30mins)**.

The view is remarkable, taking in the uninhabited Inishkea Islands and the low-lying Belmullet Peninsula. The eye is drawn from distant Benwee Head, past Slieve Fyagh, to the neighbouring dome of Slievemore on Achill Island. The Nephin Beg Mountains feature Corslieve, Glennamong, Birreencorragh and the outlying Nephin. Beyond the Minaun Heights on Achill Island you can see Corraun Hill on the mainland. Across Clew Bay is Croagh Patrick, with the Partry Mountains beyond, and the bulk of Mweelrea is also in view. Clare Island is identified by its domed hill, with Inishturk and Inishbofin adopting lower profiles. The mountains of Connemara fill the far skyline.

If you have a clear, calm day, then this is the ideal place to have lunch. On a wild and wet day there's really no shelter on the higher parts of the walk. The time allowance for this walk includes an hour for lunch.

(If you needed to cut this walk short for any reason, then you could either descend very steeply southwards to the road at Keem Bay, or descend a little less steeply south-east towards the same road, but closer to Dooagh.)

6. There are actually two summits on Croaghaun, and a clear path leads along a narrow ridge from the main summit to a subsidiary at 664m (2,192ft). This is a fine pointed peak and beyond it the ground begins to fall away more and more steeply. It is important not to rush down this slope, but to place each foot carefully and take the descent slowly and steadily. Zig-zag around boulders on the upper slopes of heather, then walk down the lower slopes of grass to reach a boggy valley drained by a little stream. Aim to land in this valley just to the right of a couple of small bog pools **(5hrs 30mins)**.

7. If you need a rapid exit from this point, then simply turn left and follow the valley down to the road at Keem Strand. To continue with the walk, however, and to experience some dramatic cliff scenery, climb straight uphill to reach the jagged crest of Benmore. The highest point is at 332m (1,089ft), but there are a handful of airy perches above the cliffs.

    Turn right to follow a path along the crest, dropping down to a narrow gap where the grass has been grazed very short. Be careful of these slopes, as they can be very slippery when wet. The traverse of Achill Head is achieved by following a trodden path and occasionally scrambling on rock. Go only as far as you feel able, as you have to retrace your steps again afterwards. Enjoy the feeling of being isolated on such an exposed rocky ridge so far out in the ocean **(6hrs)**.

8. Retracing your steps along the crest to Benmore, you can either follow the jagged cliff edge faithfully, which is like walking a range of miniature mountain summits, or use a path that manages to omit all the little points along the way. The cliff scenery is awesome throughout. The southern end of the headland is Moyteoge Head, and it is worth following a path to a ruined lookout tower, even though it means doubling back a short way afterwards.

Follow a path downhill from Moyteoge Head to reach a car park and road-end at Keem Strand. There is a little information board overlooking the sandy beach, and you can read while your knees recover from some of the punishing slopes recently endured **(7hrs)**.

9. All that remains is to follow the R319 road from Keem Strand back to Dooagh. First you zig-zag up from the beach, passing toilets and another car park. The road has been cut from the steep, rugged slopes of Croaghaun and buttressed on the lower side. There are fine views along the coast from the road, then as it starts to descend, look out for a curious feature on the right.

The word 'EIRE' has been spelt out in huge letters of stone on a coastal heath. This was done at intervals around the north-west coast of Ireland in the Second World War. It was to warn aircraft pilots not to land in neutral Ireland. Even those who landed in an emergency, or survived a crash-landing, were liable to be interned.

As the road returns to Dooagh, white houses are scattered across the landscape. There are a handful of places offering food and drink, and you pass the stone commemorating Don Allum's rowing exploits both ways across the Atlantic Ocean. A short way along the road is the Post Office where the walk started **(8hrs)**.

Other walks in the area

Achill Island is made for good walks. You could climb the huge dome of Slievemore, or walk along the top of the Minaun Cliffs, or climb any of the little hills to enjoy a good walk and fine views.

Places of interest

The deserted village on the slopes of Slievemore is a popular choice with most visitors. The gaunt ruins of long abandoned cottages are threaded by a single 'street' leading towards the mountains.

Walk 13:
Clare Island & Knockmore
A Clare Island Survey

It is easy to spot Clare Island from the mainland and from other islands. The huge hump of Knockmore, the highest hill on the island, is its most prominent feature. The island was the main base of Granuaile, the notorious 16th century sea-queen pirate who conducted campaigns both at sea and on the mainland and is said to be buried in Clare Island Abbey. You can have a look at the Abbey ruins as you walk round Clare Island, climbing over Knockmore and marvelling at the extensive views. There are dramatic cliffs too; in fact, there's easily enough to warrant staying a whole weekend so you aren't rushed off your feet.

Grade: Moderate

Distance: 18km (11 miles)

Time: 7 hours (including an hour for lunch)

Start & Finish: Beside Granuaile's Castle at the pier 715853

Map: Ordnance Survey of Ireland Discovery 30

How to get there

By car: Follow the R335 road west of Westport to reach Louisburgh. Just as you leave the village, turn right along the minor road for Roonagh Quay, where there is parking available beside the ferry offices.

By bus: Bus Éireann table number 450 is an occasional service from Westport to Louisburgh, but there are no buses to Roonagh Quay. However, you may find that local taxi/minibuses are already booked to take some people out to Roonagh Quay to tie in with the ferry services, and may be able to squeeze you in too.

By ferry: There are two ferries operating between Roonagh Quay and Clare Island, offering daily services. Phone for details on 00-353-98-26307 for the Pirate Queen and 00-353-98-25045 for O'Malleys.

Necessities: Boots as there can be rough and wet patches on the island; waterproofs as there is little shelter from rain and wind; **money** for the ferry and for food and drink on the island; the **ferry timetables** to avoid being stranded; and keep hold of your ticket!

Notes: The walk around Clare Island is wonderful. If you can manage to spend a night on the island, then you won't feel under any pressure to dash around between ferries. You can stay in a B&B, hotel, or an unusual lighthouse on a cliff edge! The view from Knockmore on a clear day is both interesting and extensive, and it is worth tackling this walk at a time when good weather is forecast.

Introduction

Granuaile, often Anglicised as Grace O'Malley, was a remarkable woman. Historical details of her life are sketchy, but local folklore has made her into a colourful, larger-than-life character. She lived for over seventy years through the turbulent times of the 16th century. She raided passing ships from her castles and harbours on Clare Island, Achill Island and Inishbofin. She had other castles on the mainland and was embroiled in all kinds of skirmishes. It is known that she sailed to London and was pardoned by Queen Elizabeth, even gaining permission to legitimise her piracy under the guise of harrying the Queen's enemies! She overshadowed and overruled her husbands. These are the plain facts, beyond which folklore and legend have created an even more amazing woman. It is thought

The attractive lighthouse at the northern end of Clare Island

that she is buried in Clare Island Abbey, which is only a small foundation, but noted for its wall paintings.

Spend any amount of time on Clare Island and you'll find some mention of the 'Clare Island Survey'. This took place between the years 1909-11, when natural historians and academics took lodgings on the island and scrutinised every feature of the landscape, drawing up comprehensive lists of plants and animals. They found the time to meet with the islanders and learn from them, taking copious notes and stories from them.

The results of the survey were published in a huge volume, which many of the islanders still cherish in their homes, but is otherwise something you'd have great difficulty trying to obtain. The introduction states: *'The selection of Clare Island was influenced by its suitable size, position and unusual elevation as compared with most of the western islands; it lay sufficiently off the coast to raise interesting problems as to the immigration of its flora and fauna, but not so far as to introduce delay and expense to the working parties owing to precarious communication with the mainland.'*

You may not choose to survey Clare Island quite so thoroughly, but you should still aim to be leisurely in your appreciation of the place, and once again it is recommended that you do at least try and stay overnight on the island. If you do try and complete the walk between the first and last ferries, please be absolutely sure of the ferry timetables.

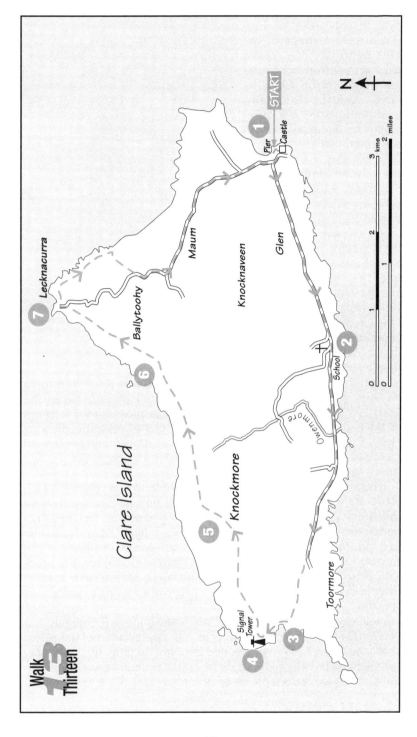

The Walk

Roonagh Quay is a pretty bleak place, but you have to make your way there and stand on the pier until one of the ferries takes you across to Clare Island. If you plan to spend a night on the island, then you should drop off your luggage at your accommodation first and maybe aim to explore just one part of the route. The walk takes most of the day to accomplish though you could structure it to take an afternoon and a morning.

1. Ferries berth at a pier on Clare Island that is overshadowed by the stout stone remains of Granuaile's Castle. Follow a narrow road inland, and unless you aim to get something to eat and drink first, turn left at a junction beside a telephone box. The road rises gently without particularly good views, but within a short while you can look across the sea to the mountains of Connemara. The road reaches a junction where there is a little shop near the Abbey and church **(1hr)**.

   It is worth spending a while wandering around the Abbey ruins and looking at some of the old gravestones. If Granuaile is indeed buried in the Abbey, then her descendents, the O'Malley's are represented in the graveyard. Study the ancient cross-slab and take note of the more recent memorial to Canadian airmen who were killed during the Second World War when their plane crashed on Knockmore.

2. Keep following the road ever westwards until you reach O'Malley's B&B near the end of the tarmac. (If you happen to choose this B&B as your base on the island, then you should get a lift to this point and therefore start reading the route directions from here.) Just opposite the B&B a track climbs uphill, passing one last house to reach a wide-open, closely-cropped grassland above some remarkable cliffs. Take care, as the cliff edge appears rather suddenly **(2hrs)**.

   There are often good thermals around the rocky coves and cliffs, so watch out for birds such as fulmars and choughs making sport on the updraught.

3. Turn right to follow the cliff line up to a ruined signal tower. The tower was linked by line of sight to one on Achill Island and another on the highest part of Inishturk **(2hrs 15mins)**.

4. Cross a little gap and start climbing onto the slopes of Knockmore. The short grass bears a few outcrops of rock and boulders, but these are easily side-stepped. Views improve all the time as height is gained. The first summit is peaty underfoot, while the second summit, is crowned by a huge cairn. There is a trig point at 462m (1,520ft) and this is the highest point on Clare Island **(3hrs 15mins)**.

Views commence with Achill Head and take in Croaghaun and Slievemore on Achill Island. The southernmost parts of Achill are quite close to Clare Island. Corraun Hill and the Nephin Beg Range lead the eye to the more distant Croaghmoyle and the Ox Mountains. Croagh Patrick's conical shape is closer to hand across Clew Bay. Next are the Sheeffry Hills, Ben Gorm, Mweelrea, the Twelve Bens of Connemara and distant Errisbeg Mountain. Rugged peninsulas and small islands spread across the sea towards Inishturk and Inishbofin.

With such an extensive and absorbing view, could there be a better place to have lunch in clear weather? The time stated for completing the walk includes an hour spent on top of Knockmore. Better be prepared for a sea breeze on top!

5. As you walk downhill from Knockmore, you'll see that the cliff-line leading towards the lighthouse on the northern point of the island is something of a roller-coaster. There is a steep descent, followed by a series of ups and downs, some of which are steep, but quite short. The grassy slopes can be slippery when wet, and you need to be careful of the cliff edge, though most of the time there is a fence. There is some outcropping rock along the way that is best avoided **(5hrs 15mins)**.

6. On the lowest gap, you need to cross a junction of fences and climb again. As you approach the lighthouse, which is in a wonderfully exposed position, don't neglect to look back over your shoulder at the towering dome of Knockmore. Aim for the lighthouse, which is served by a rough and stony track **(5hrs 45mins)**.

The lighthouse offers accommodation, and must be one of the most unusual places you could stay in Ireland. (If you stay here, then you'll probably be given a lift up the rugged road from the pier, so you can read your route description around the island from this point.)

Cross over the lighthouse access road and take a peek over the cliffs on the far side of the boundary wall. There is an area of sea off the northern point of Clare Island that's often in a state of turbulence owing to a submerged peak of rock. It is said to be particularly rich in marine life, though local fishermen keep well clear of it.

7. Continue walking along the cliffs until a small harbour is reached. At this point, the coastline ahead is divided by awkward fences and walls, so follow a track inland to return to the lighthouse access road again. Turn left and follow this onto a tarmac road, which finally leads back to the pier **(7hrs)**.

The Bay Hotel is off to the left before you reach the pier. It offers accommodation, food and drink at the eastern end of the island. If you have any time to spare before catching the ferry back to the mainland, then you could enjoy a meal or drink, then stroll down to the pier later, but keep a careful check on the ferry timetable.

Other walks in the area

As you explore most of the coast of Clare Island on this walk, there isn't much left to cover! However, there's an interesting old road crossing the island between the Abbey and the Lighthouse, which is worth following.

Places of interest

Granuaile's Castle isn't open to visitors, but you can look at it from the pier. The Abbey ruins are interesting for their wall paintings, and for the cross slab outside.

Walk 14:
Murrisk, Croagh Patrick & Leckanvey
A barefoot penitential pilgrimage

Croagh Patrick is Ireland's Holy Mountain, locally known as 'The Reek', drawing thousands of people from all over the world to climb its slopes. The stark pyramid of bright quartzite dominates the surrounding countryside and a tiny white dot catching the sun on the summit turns out to be a chapel. Pilgrims have climbed The Reek since the time of the Druids and St. Patrick fasted on the summit forty days and nights. Some people, out of a sense of devotion, climb the mountain in their bare feet, while on the last Sunday in July, 'Reek Sunday', tens of thousands flock to the mountain and work their way round the penitential 'stations' for the good of their souls. The circuit offered here uses the main pilgrim trail to the summit, taking in all the 'stations', then descends to Leckanvey and follows the road back to Murrisk.

Grade: Strenuous

Distance: 11km (7 miles)

Time: 5 hours (including an hour for lunch or at the pub)

Start & Finish: Park at the large car park at Murrisk 920823

Maps: Ordnance Survey of Ireland Discovery 30, 31, 37 & 38

How to get there

By car: Drive westwards from Westport along the R335 road towards Louisburgh. Large signs announce Murrisk, Croagh Patrick and the National Famine Monument. Park at the large car park near Campbell's Bar at Murrisk.

By bus: While there are plenty of Bus Éireann services to and from Westport, there are only a few between Westport and Murrisk. Check Bus Éireann table number 450 carefully to be sure you can get out and back using the buses.

Necessities: Boots as the slopes are steep and stony; **waterproofs** as the mountain is very exposed; **food and drink** as the climb is strenuous; **money** for a drink at one of the pubs; **bus timetables** for the limited service on the road; the **weather forecast** should be a good one if you want good views; **extra sticking plasters** in case you find some barefoot pilgrim in need of first aid.

Notes: This must be the most popular mountain in the whole of Ireland. Every day, and in almost every weather, someone manages to reach the summit, but it can be a rough, tough treadmill in foul weather. If you are lucky enough to climb The Reek on a clear day, then you can enjoy superb views of Connemara and Clew Bay, a spread of islands and the bleak Nephin Beg Range. As Ireland's Holy Mountain, this is a special place, and with a bit of luck you'll be able to savour the peculiar spiritual ambience of The Reek.

A pilgrim with staff in hand reaches the stony summit

Introduction

Croagh Patrick has always been a sacred mountain. To the Druids it was *Cruachan Aigle*, and they constructed a 30km (19 mile) trail to the summit, traces of which still survive after 2,000 years. St. Patrick followed the Druidical trail with his charioteer Benain in the year 441. While Benain waited on the shoulder of the mountain, St. Patrick went to the summit to pray and fast for forty days and nights. Coming down from the mountain, he cast all the snakes out of Ireland. Finding his charioteer dead, he built a cairn over the body and decreed that it would ever afterwards be a place of pilgrimage.

Recent excavations led by Ireland's renowned archaeologist Michael Gibbons produced several surprises on the summit of Croagh Patrick. Not only were the foundations of an ancient church exposed, but it was discovered to be the oldest church in Ireland. Furthermore, glass beads were discovered from the 3rd century, and the entire summit is encircled by the ramparts of an Iron Age fort. There are also hut circles just off the summit which date back well over 2000 years, offering even more evidence of the reverence that has been bestowed on the mountain throughout the ages. When workable deposits of gold were found in the bedrock, the Government banned all exploitation, deeming it inappropriate for Ireland's Holy Mountain.

There are occasional guided walks along the old Druidical trail from Ballintubber Abbey to the summit of Croagh Patrick, but most people climbing The Reek do it on a well worn path from Murrisk. At the foot of the mountain is a statue of St. Patrick and a plaque stating the 'rules' for the pilgrimage. Apart from 'Reek Sunday', the last Sunday in July, you'll find that most people climb the mountain simply for a good walk. All the same, you will pass the pilgrimage 'stations' on the following walk.

The idea is to climb The Reek from Murrisk, taking things steadily on the steep and worn path, and especially taking care on the loose scree towards the summit. In good weather it is well worth spending an hour or so on top, then the route moves down the other side to descend to Leckanvey. There is a road-walk back to Murrisk, where other items of interest include the ruins of Murrisk Abbey and the more recent 'ship of bones' sculpture which is Ireland's National Famine Monument.

The Walk

Use the large car park at Murrisk, which is just off the R335 road near Campbell's Bar. There are toilets . Expect this car park to be quite busy in the summer, and expect to have no hope to park your car here on the last Sunday in July!

1. Starting from the car park at Murrisk, there is a narrow road just behind the toilets, and this leads uphill past a few houses. A little sign at the end of the road reminds you that the mountain can be dangerous, and a worn-out slope leads up to a statue of St. Patrick. At this point you could pause and read the 'rules' of the pilgrimage, outlining the prayers and rituals required at three 'stations' on the mountain **(10mins)**.

2. The path beyond the statue is quite obvious, being broad and stony, and you can see it rising almost all the way to the conical summit of the mountain. The first stages of the route lead you up around a heather hollow and gradually up to the skyline ahead, where you swing to the right along a knobbly shoulder of the mountain. There are toilets off to the left, not something you expect to see at 480 metres (1,575 feet), but this is no ordinary mountain walk **(1hr)**.

3. You can catch your breath on the shoulder, as the gradient is easier. You reach a cairn called Leacht Benain, where St. Patrick's charioteer died and was buried. This is one of the traditional 'stations' on the pilgrimage, where prayers are said while walking around the cairn. You may well breathe a prayer when you see the steep slope of quartzite scree rising ahead of you. Lean into the slope, try not to wear yourself out by rushing up the loose stones, and in time you will reach the summit of Croagh Patrick **(1 hr 45mins)**.

   The whitewashed chapel on the summit is the most obvious feature, along with more toilets, which are a bonus at 764 metres (2510 feet)! Other structures may leave you wondering, but if you climb The

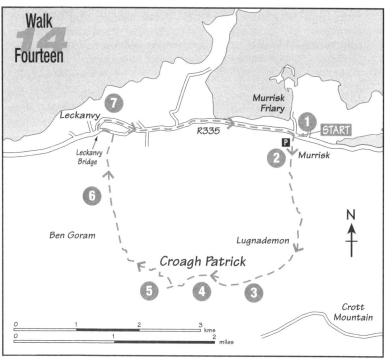

Reek on the last Sunday in July, you'll realise that they are souvenir stalls. It takes an amount of detective work to trace the ramparts of the Iron Age fort around the summit, and the place where Ireland's oldest church was excavated was cunningly back-filled to deter vandalism. If you can obtain a photograph of the excavation, you'll be able to pinpoint its location. You'll notice St. Patrick's Bed, which is another 'station' on the pilgrimage. Take your time if the day is clear; you're given a full hour in the time allowance to enjoy your lunch and have a good look around.

On a clear day, the summit structures are secondary to the view, which can be truly extensive. With luck you'll be able to see across the island-studded Clew Bay to the Nephin Beg Range and Achill Island. Clare Island is also prominent out to sea. Looking inland, you can see mighty Mweelrea, the Mountains of Connemara and the broad plateau of Maumtrasna.

4. If you want to retrace your steps to Murrisk, then by all means do so, but it can be tiresome having to tell all the people still climbing the mountain how far it is to the top! Better to continue along the crest of The Reek, following a stony path roughly westwards. Zig-zags lead you down to a shoulder where a huddle of cairns is known as Roilig Mhuire. This is the final 'station' on the pilgrimage **(3hrs 15mins)**.

Although the pilgrimage is Christian, it is quite likely that the cairns are Bronze Age burial sites. In past centuries, pilgrims would have continued even further westwards, leaving the Irish mainland and performing further rituals on Caher Island, where there was a monastic community based.

5. You need to retrace your steps a little from the cairns, then follow another zig-zag path further downhill. The stony, heathery slope is quite steep and you need to take care on loose stones. The path wanders downhill alongside a stream at a gentler gradient. When the stream reaches a low drystone wall, simply step across (**3hrs 45mins**).

6. Continue across an enclosed moorland dotted with thorny scrub. You don't have to cross any more walls and fences as a path weaves through the scrub and a track leads to a gate giving access to a minor road at Leckanvey. You could turn right and head straight back towards Murrisk, but you might like to turn left to reach Staunton's Bar for a refreshing drink (**4hrs**).

   Note that the timing doesn't include a break at Staunton's, so keep an eye on your watch, especially if you are hoping to catch a bus back to Westport!

7. Leaving Leckanvey, you'll notice St. Patrick's church set a little way back from the R335 road. When pilgrims are too old or too ill to climb Croagh Patrick, they are permitted to pray in this church and achieve the same merits.

   Follow the road directly eastwards to return to Murrisk. You'll pass a large sign on the way stating that Croagh Patrick and the National Famine Monument are ahead. At the halfway point you might just notice the shore of Clew Bay off the side of the road. The road leads back to Murrisk, where it is worth having a wander around if you still have a few minutes to spare (**5hrs**).

   The Famine Monument is in the shape of a huge bronze sculpture; a 'ship of bones' to represent the 'coffin ships' that carried so many Irish emigrants away from these shores in the middle of the 19th century. You can also walk down the nearby lane to have a look at the ruins of Murrisk Friary, or cross the road and retire to Campbell's Bar for a drink.

Other walks in the area

The waymarked Western Way crosses the shoulder of Croagh Patrick and passes through Westport, offering some easy low-level walking. Obtain a copy of the Western Way guidebook for details. There are also guided pilgrimage walks to Croagh Patrick from Ballintubber Abbey, following what was once a Druidical causeway.

Places of interest

Westport House is the big attraction in Westport. Less well known is the Croagh Patrick Exhibition at the Club Atlantic Hostel.

Walk 15:
Mweelrea from Delphi Bridge
The highest mountain in Connacht

There are no easy ways up Mweelrea; only difficult ways and more difficult ways. Mweelrea is the highest mountain in the Province of Connacht, so you can't really expect anything other than an arduous walk. The ascent from Delphi is difficult, but otherwise fairly straightforward. A broad and boggy valley gives way to steep and rugged slopes. The high summits are rather easier to traverse, but need great care in mist. There is a long ridge leading back into the boggy valley at the end of the day. On a fine day, with plenty of time on your side, it is a memorable mountain walk, but in bad weather is best left well alone. Mweelrea is best climbed for its extensive views, so you should reserve a good, clear, dry day for the walk.

Grade: Strenuous

Distance: 16km (10 miles)

Time: 6½ hours (including an hour for lunch)

Start & Finish: Delphi Bridge 841652

Map: Ordnance Survey of Ireland Discovery 37

How to get there
> *By car:* Delphi can be approached from Louisburgh and the Doo Lough Pass via the R335 road, or from Leenane and Killary Harbour via the main N59 road and R335 road. There is not much parking available beside the road near Delphi Bridge, and if you use the car park at the Delphi Adventure Centre you should ask for permission first.
> *By bus:* There are no bus services to Delphi.

Necessities: Boots as the ground can be very wet and boggy; **waterproofs** as the mountain is very exposed; **compass** as mist can make the ridges difficult to follow; **food and drink** as there are no places to obtain these on the walk.

Notes: Make no mistake; the ascent of Mweelrea is a difficult undertaking. Ground conditions are often wet and boggy, and the steep slopes can be slippery in places. If you find the lower slopes hard going, don't be afraid to turn back before it is too late.

Introduction

Mweelrea is head and shoulders above all other mountains in the Province of Connacht. Its southern slopes fall steep and rugged into the sea at Killary Harbour, while its northern slopes fall steep and rocky towards the Doo Lough Pass. It seems that ascents from most sides are steep, rugged and difficult underfoot. It is best for first-time visitors to avoid the Doo Lough side of the mountain altogether. An ascent from Delphi exploits a broad and boggy valley at first, but there's no avoiding steep and rugged climbing later. Once the summit of this

Mweelrea towers above the head of a boggy, bouldery glen

mighty mountain has been gained, however, it is actually fairly easy to link the other high summits on a clear day. In mist you'd need to take more care, and you'd certainly need to be very careful to identify the correct line of descent. Some of the slopes are really very steep and others are far too rocky to descend safely.

There is an exclusive fishing lodge at Delphi, and anyone driving to it from Louisburgh will notice a couple of stone memorial crosses in prominent positions near the road. They recall an event from the dark days of the Great Famine that is remembered as the Doolough Tragedy. It happened that a number of gentlemen charged with administering famine relief were staying at Delphi in March 1849.

News reached the starving populace around Louisburgh, and in a rising storm they set out to walk to Delphi in the hope of procuring food. They were turned away from the door, and on the way back through the Doolough Pass, the storm rose against them. Many died of exposure during the night, some were blown into the lough and drowned, and others died through sicknesses they endured as a result of the journey in the cold and wet. The Doolough Tragedy is commemorated in an annual walk between Louisburgh and Delphi, often with politicians and overseas aid organisations represented.

The Walk

There is no parking beside Delphi Bridge, so either pick a convenient space beside the R335 road, or ask for permission to park at the nearby Delphi Adventure Centre. Patrons of the nearby Delphi Lodge could complete the walk from that establishment on foot.

1. Starting at the lovely stone arch of Delphi Bridge, go through an iron gate close to the bridge and follow a short track flanked by rhododendron bushes. This leads to a footbridge and a house, but you don't cross the bridge or reach the house. Instead, walk upstream beside the Owenaglogh River, crossing a squelchy, boggy area. You walk on a boggy strip between a forest fence and the river. You might be tempted to cross the fence and follow a forest track a short way, but you'll have to cross back again later, so it's hardly worth the bother. You reach a far corner of the forest after passing a couple of activity sites associated with the Delphi Adventure Centre **(30mins)**.

   You seem to be surrounded by mountains; towering great mountains. Mweelrea is at the head of the glen, and some of its nameless shoulders truly dominate the glen. The rugged summits of Ben Creggan and Ben Gorm are seen when you look back downstream.

2. Cross a stretch of open, tussocky bogland, then walk on another boggy strip between another forest fence and the river. There are some small waterfalls in the river, attractively adorned with a few holly trees. When you leave the far corner of the forest, cross another expanse of tussocky bog to reach a younger forest plantation. After that, you're in the wilderness head of the valley, beneath the rugged face of Mweelrea **(1hr 30mins)**.

3. Walk gradually up a boggy, tussocky slope scattered with huge boulders. You should aim for a gap on the skyline to the left of Mweelrea. You walk roughly parallel to a stream called the Sruhaunbunatrench, which flows from a hidden pool called Lough Lugaloughan. There is no need to walk too close to the watercourse, so you can pick any line that seems best to reach the gap. You'll cross a tongue of debris that was washed out of a gully, then the ground steepens as you finally ascend to the gap **(2hrs 15mins)**.

   Views begin to open up now that you're free from the confines of the glen. You can look down on little Lough Lugaloughan, which is remarkably shallow, and boulders protrude from the very centre of the pool. Looking over the other side of the gap, you see the long sea inlet of Killary Harbour, with range upon range of mountains beyond.

4. Climb steeply uphill from the gap. It really is steep in places, and you may need to clutch frantically at tufts of grass in a few places. The slope eases a little at a higher level, and there are some points

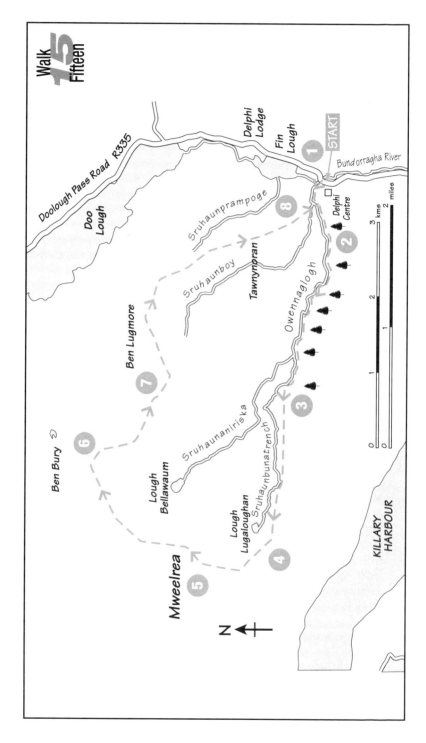

where you can stand on level ground and take a breather. There are dark, damp buttresses and gullies off to the right, and it is worth looking back over your shoulder from time to time as these often look more dramatic once you've passed them. The summit of Mweelrea rises to 814m (2,688ft), where a cairn sits on a dome of blanket bog **(3hrs)**.

In clear weather, spend a while observing the extensive panorama. Out to sea are Inishbofin, Inishturk, Clare Island and Achill Island. Corraun Hill and the Nephin Beg Range lead the eye inland to Nephin and Croagh Patrick. Looking past the nearby summits you see the Sheeffry Hills, Ben Creggan and Ben Gorm. Maumtrasna's high plateau is followed by the Devilsmother and the hills of Joyce Country. Leenane and Leenane Hill are followed by the Maum Turk Mountains and the Twelve Bens. Doughruagh, Diamond Hill and Tully Mountain lead the eye back round to the sea.

On a clear, calm day the summit makes a fine perch for lunch while you survey the distant ranges of mountains. If you choose to take a break here on top of the world, then the time given for the walk includes an hour for lunch. In bad weather there's little shelter on the summit or anywhere nearby.

5. Walk down a stony, grassy slope, with low outcrops of rock, and cross a broad gap. Climb up a grassy, stony slope, aiming for what appears to be a summit cairn. It isn't, but if you swing right and continue climbing gently along a stony crest, then you'll reach the summit of Ben Bury at 795m (2,610ft), and there's a cairn on top **(4hrs 45mins)**.

From this point, the distant mountains of Nephin and Croagh Patrick look like twin breasts, but are actually quite far a apart and wouldn't look the same if they were side by side.

6. Walk down to a little gap overlooking the huge hollow of Lugmore, with Doo Lough far below. There is a cairn on the gap, and walkers do sometimes climb up and down the mountain via Lugmore, but it is steep, rocky and dangerous. Walk up a stony, grassy slope and cross a fairly gentle summit. As you follow the ridge further along, it becomes quite narrow and rocky, as well as jagged and sharp in places. There is a fairly well trodden path, then you drop down a bouldery slope to cross another little gap, and climb a bouldery slope to reach the top of Ben Lugmore. The height is 803m (2,635ft), and in mist it can be difficult to distinguish this point from other humps and bumps on the ridge **(5hrs 15mins)**.

7. Walk down a bouldery slope to leave Ben Lugmore, crossing another little gap and climbing a grassy slope to reach the next summit. It is a fairly broad and grassy place bearing a little cairn.

Continue along the ridge, then descend in stages along a rather rugged, blunt sort of ridge. There is a path in places, but also areas of wet ground and low outcrops of rock. Tread with care as the ground can be slippery, and make your way down to the lower, tussocky bog in the bottom of the glen. You'll find that vague paths lead to a turf bank, and if you follow this, then a fence will lead you onwards to a stream (**6hrs 15mins**).

8. Cross over the stream, then cross over the Owenaglogh River, which is rather wider and carries more water. There are plenty of boulders to use as stepping stones, or you could choose to jump across a more constricted rocky part of the river. Either way, the aim is to get to the other side. (If flooding prevents an easy ford, then you could walk downstream to a house and cross a footbridge.) Once you gain the far bank, turn left and walk downstream across a rather wet and boggy area. You covered this stretch at the start of the day's walk, and you'll link with the track flanked by rhododendron bushes, which will lead you back to the road near Delphi Bridge (**6hrs 30mins**).

Other walks in the area

There are plenty of mountains in the area, including the Sheeffry Hills and Ben Gorm, which rise just as precipitously from the shores of Doo Lough as Mweelrea, Ben Bury and Ben Lugmore.

Places of interest

The Granuaile Interpretive Centre at Louisburgh is worth visiting, as well as the Leenane Cultural Centre on the other side of Killary Harbour at Leenane.

Walk 16:
Killary Harbour coastal walk
Walking by water

Killary Harbour is a remarkable sea inlet. It has been described as Ireland's only true fjord; carved by glaciers and deeper along parts of its length than it is at its mouth. In fact, the mouth of the fjord is almost blocked by a rugged little island. The mighty mountains of Mweelrea and Ben Gorm dominate the northern side of Killary Harbour, while the Devilsmother, Leenane Hill and the rugged little hill called Binn Mhór rise on the southern side of the inlet. There is an old famine road on the southern side and you can follow it from Bunowen to Killary Harbour Youth Hostel, enjoying a fine coastal walk. For the return journey you can follow minor roads inland, passing Lough Muck and Lough Fee to maintain the watery theme as you complete the circuit.

Grade: Easy

Distance: 16km (10 miles)

Time: 6 hours (including an hour for lunch)

Start & Finish: At a junction of the N59 and the road to Bunowen 821607

Maps: Ordnance Survey of Ireland Discovery 37 and Harveys Superwalker Map of Connemara

How to get there
By car: The road for Bunowen lies off the main N59 road between Leenane and Kylemore. The turning is signposted as the Connemara Way in Irish: 'Bealach na Gaeltachta Slí Chonamara'. A stone beside the road junction confirms that this is the road for Bunowen. You can't park at this junction, but there is a space where gravel is stored just round the bend in the direction of Leenane.
By bus: Bus Éireann table number 61 between Westport and Clifden runs along the main N59 road in summer. The only other service is the occasional table number 419 service between Clifden and Galway on Tuesday and Saturday.

Necessities: Walking shoes will suffice in dry weather; **waterproofs** if rain is forecast; **food and drink** as there is nothing along the way.

Notes: This is a relatively easy walk. Many walkers choose it as a wet-weather option when they don't feel like climbing the mountains, but it is actually a good walk to do on a clear, dry day as the colours can be quite remarkable. A farm road and an old track are followed to Killary Harbour Youth Hostel, then minor roads lead back to the start. You could complete this circuit in walking shoes rather than boots if the ground is dry.

Introduction

The coastal walk on the southern side of Killary Harbour is quite popular, but is by no means overrun with walkers. It has been included in the long distance waymarked trail called the Connemara Way and it

An optional circuit leads around the little Lough Muck

offers a pleasant walk to anyone staying at Killary Harbour Youth Hostel. The hostel was formerly called Rosroe Cottage. The philosopher Ludwig Wittgenstein lived and worked there in 1948. Lobster pots and boats often surround the little harbour alongside.

In 1903 the British naval fleet anchored at Killary while King Edward VIII and Queen Alexandra made a sightseeing tour of Connemara and visited nearby Kylemore, where the Gothic extravaganza of Kylemore Castle had already been built. A few years earlier, in 1853, Dr. William Wilde had a house called Illaunroe built beside Lough Fee. His son, who became the noted playwright Oscar Wilde, stayed in the house in the years 1876-8 and enjoyed fishing on the lake.

Before the area became popular with tourists, the population was stricken during the Great Famine. Part of the route you follow is based on a famine relief road and though it is grass-grown and has never seen much traffic, you'll see that it was also well engineered across a steep and rugged slope. You can see roofless ruins, fields and old cultivation ridges around the abandoned settlement of Foher. Above Foher is a rugged gap in the hills known as Salrock Pass, and you'll see it from both sides on this walk. According to legend, the gap was formed when the Devil dragged the local St. Roc over the hills with a chain. It is also said that smugglers landing contraband at Little Killary used to carry it over the Salrock Pass, along the shore of Killary Harbour and inland for further distribution.

In recent years the calm waters of Killary Harbour have been filled with fishery structures. There are fish cages and mussel rafts at intervals between Leenane and the mouth of the inlet. You'll pass one of the boat slips used to service these structures, and beyond Killary Harbour Youth Hostel there is another fishery development. The most recent development is the provision of cruising trips along the length of the inlet. You could use one of these voyages to get a preview of the coastal walk.

The Walk

When you've located the start of this walk, remember to park nearby on the space where gravel is stored, rather than risk obstructing the road junction itself. If you're arriving by bus, keep an eye on your map and give the driver due notice when you want to get off.

1. The minor road leaves the main N59 road and is signposted as 'Bealach na Gaeltachta Slí Chonamara'. A stone at the side of the road is marked 'Bunowen'. As you follow the road downhill past turf cuttings, you'll see the stumps and roots of ancient bog pines have been exposed. The whole area was once covered in pines. The road overlooks a wooded valley where the Bunowen River rushes down towards Killary Harbour, while ahead rises the great bulk of Mweelrea on the other side of the inlet. Pass a couple of houses and farm buildings, then go through a gate on a gentle rise on the road (**30mins**).

2. The tarmac gives way to a broad gravel track running gently down across a rugged moorland slope. There is a house just beyond a small conifer plantation, as well as a boathouse and slipway on the shore which are associated with the fishery enterprises in Killary Harbour. Cross a stile beside a gate to continue along the track (**1hr**).

3. When you reach another gate and cross another stile, you immediately cross a concrete slab bridge where a small waterfall pours into Killary Harbour from the steep slopes of Binn Mhór. This can be quite impressive after heavy rain. The track becomes grassier and has a low, ruined, drystone wall to the right. As you walk further, you go through a gate in a drystone wall, then continue with a drystone wall and fence on the right to reach a cottage at Foher (**1hr 20mins**).

There is a cottage at Foher, and another one further uphill, as well as roofless grey ruins scattered across a slope that was obviously quite fertile in its time. The lines of old potato ridges can be seen, and it was the depredations of the Great Famine that led to this little settlement being abandoned. High above Foher you can see the rugged little gap of the Salrock Pass, where the Devil tried to drag St. Roc over the mountain.

4. Walk further along the grassy track and go through an iron gate in a wall, then cross a stile over the next wall. There is a short, steep climb where the track negotiates a cliff face. See how the track was buttressed with a retaining wall to ensure it stayed in position. There is a rough, boggy slope beyond and while some parts have degenerated into a narrow path, the line of the old track is clear to follow without difficulty. The track is diverted away from Killary Harbour by a wall, and you'll find yourself led to a cottage and a minor road. Turn right to follow the road to Killary Harbour Youth Hostel (**2hrs**).

The hostel, formerly Rosroe Cottage, was used by the philosopher Ludwig Wittgenstein in 1948, and a plaque on the wall recalls his brief occupancy.

The little harbour alongside can be a good place to take a lunch break. The time allowance for the walk assumes you'll spend an hour at this point, though you could continue the walk further before taking a break.

5. Follow the minor road inland from the hostel and harbour, passing a few cottages on the way. The road runs alongside the sea inlet of Little Killary, climbing a short way to offer good views towards the wooded head of the inlet. The road runs downhill, then climbs past the driveways for the Little Killary Centre and Salrock House. Follow the road uphill from the woods and continue straight onwards at a junction. The road drops down to the shore of little Lough Muck, where you turn left (**4hrs**).

You could, at this point, embark on a short circular walk around Lough Muck. If you choose to do this, then give yourself another hour as it is about 3km (2 miles) around the shore. Follow the road through a gap, then follow the farm track on the right. Go through a gate, then turn sharply right to walk alongside a fence. After passing a junction with another fence, you could climb uphill a short way to see a circular stone cashel in a fine defensive position and a commanding view over the rugged pass between Lough Muck and Lough Fee. Continue walking along the shore of Lough Muck to reach the outflowing Culfin River. Cross the river using a wooden footbridge, then turn right to follow a road past a small white chapel. Continue along the road, passing a couple of houses in wooded surroundings, then walk back to the road junction where you started this little circular diversion.

6. If you don't want to walk around Lough Muck, then simply follow the minor road straight through the gap to reach Lough Fee. The road hugs the shore of the lough and passes a few little farmhouses. There is a wooded promontory where Dr. William Wilde built the house called Illaunroe, and you walk past this point by road (**4hrs 30mins**).

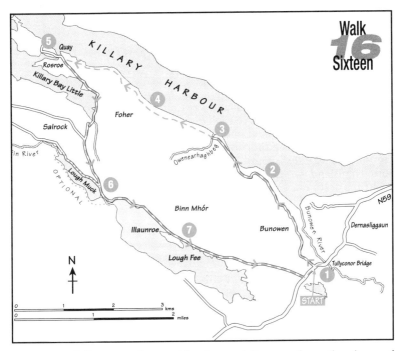

Walk Sixteen 16

7. Beyond Illaunroe the road begins to drift away from the shore of Lough Fee, climbing gently up a broad and boggy slope. You can see the Maum Turk Mountains ahead and the Twelve Bens off to the right; both ranges being somewhat distant. When the minor road reaches the main N59 road, turn left to return to the road junction where you started. If you parked your car in the space where gravel is stored, then follow the road a little further to return to that point.

    This stretch of the road seems to be in the middle of nowhere and can be a bleak place when the rain is lashing down. If you are looking for food and drink nearby, then you'll have to head either for Leenane or Kylemore along the main N59 road, or Lough Inagh Lodge on the R344 road

Other walks in the area

You could adapt this walk by climbing the rugged little hill called Binn Mhór, instead of following the road at the end, or you could make the hill the subject of another walk altogether. Benchoona is also worth climbing in this area.

Places of interest

There is little to see in the immediate surroundings, but if you're travelling on the main road towards Kylemore, the award-winning modern Creevagh Church is worth inspecting.

Walk 17:
A circuit of Inishbofin
Exploring a pirate haven

On a map Inishbofin looks quite small, but its coastline is amazingly indented. If you wish to walk all the way round the coast, expect it to take all day. A succession of rugged headlands, sandy bays and rocky coves ensure constant variety and interest. As you approach Inishbofin, you'll appreciate that it has a fine, long, sheltered natural harbour, and you'll see that the harbour mouth is guarded by the star-shaped Cromwell's Fort. The island was once home to a monastic community, was once a base for a notorious band of pirates, and was once a gruesome prison for captured priests during the Cromwellian campaign.

Grade: Moderate

Distance: 23km (14 miles)

Time: 7½ hours (including an hour for lunch)

Start & Finish: On the pier in Bofin Harbour 536648

Maps: Ordnance Survey of Ireland Discovery 37.

How to get there

> *By car:* Cleggan is signposted from the N59 road north of Clifden. The usual approach to the village is from a road junction in the middle of a broad bog, where half a dozen colourful signs beg you to visit. Park near the harbour.
>
> *By bus:* Michael Nee's Bus runs daily between Clifden and Cleggan, linking with the ferry service to and from Inishbofin. Bus Éireann table number 422 serves Cleggan on Wednesdays.
>
> *By ferry:* There are daily ferry services to Inishbofin from Cleggan, operated by King's and the Dun Aengus Mailboat. There are ferry enquiry and booking offices in Clifden and Cleggan, or you can phone for details on 095-44750.

Necessities: *Boots as some parts of the island can be wet and muddy; waterproofs if rain is forecast; bus and/or ferry timetables if you don't want to be marooned; food and drink for the walk; money for food and drink in one of the island hotels.*

Notes: This is a relatively easy walk, but there are parts of the island that can be wet, muddy or rugged. You need to take care when walking near cliffs and rocky coves, especially in foul weather. In good weather you will be tempted to linger and enjoy the spectacular scenery, so it is better to stay overnight on the island to be sure of having plenty of time available. If you do need to cut the walk short, refer to your map to spot obvious paths and tracks across the island.

Introduction

Inishbofin is a remarkably scenic and interesting little island, and is becoming more and more popular. The ferry journey allows you to

Bofin Harbour is a lovely, calm, natural harbour on the island

study the southern coast in some detail. You also see green fields and little farms, giving the impression that this is a fertile island. Far from it; much of the island is in fact bleak and barren. The northern and western cliffs are truly spectacular, riven by rocky coves, with headlands battered by the full force of the Atlantic Ocean. There are rock stacks, rock arches and an intriguing subterranean passage.

A wealth of archaeological remains abound on Inishbofin, and you can roll back the centuries while studying them. The star-shaped fort known as Cromwell's Fort once boasted 24 cannons and although now in ruins, the structure remains an imposing sight at the harbour mouth. The fort was built after the island surrendered to Cromwellian troops at the very end of the Civil War in 1653. Irish priests were rounded up and despatched to the rock arch known as The Prison on the island; many of them dying there while awaiting transportation up until the year 1660.

The Spanish pirate Don Bosco constructed an earlier fort at the harbour mouth. He was a contemporary of the legendary Irish sea-queen Granuaile. The O'Malley family held the island from 1380 to 1603 and Granuaile was their most colourful character. According to local lore, she considered herself a queen equal to Elizabeth I. Whatever the truth, she was certainly given leave to harry the Queen's enemies off the Irish coast; nothing more than legitimising the piracy she was already wont to practice!

Centuries earlier, St.Colman and a band of thirty monks settled on Inishbofin in the year 665. They left Lindisfarne off the English coast in

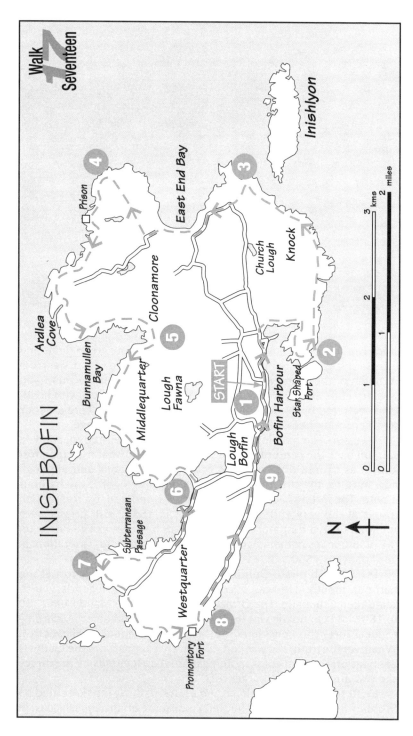

INISHBOFIN

Walk Seventeen

Inishlyon

East End Bay

Prison

Ardlea Cove

Cloonamore

Bunnamullen Bay

Church Lough

Knock

Middlequarter

Lough Fawna

START

Bofin Harbour

Star Shaped Fort

Lough Bofin

Subterranean Passage

Westquarter

Promontory Fort

N

0   1   2   3 kms
0   1   2 miles

a fury after the Synod of Whitby set new rules governing the date of Easter. Colman founded an Abbey on the eastern side of Inishbofin, though the ruins you see today date from the 14th century. The Abbey was used up until the 16th century.

If you delve even further back into Inishbofin's history you'll find a host of archaeological remains on the island, from promontory forts on battered headlands to ancient field boundaries buries beneath the bog. In fact, there's so much to see on Inishbofin that you should consider spending a couple of nights there and exploring the island in as much detail as possible.

The Walk

No matter how much of a swell there is on the crossing, the sheltered inlet of Bofin Harbour is generally calm. If you're only here for the day, then you'd better get moving, but if you're staying on the island, then you can enjoy it at your leisure.

1. Leave the pier and turn right to follow the road round Bofin Harbour, passing the church to reach Day's Hotel. You could take a break here for a drink and a snack, or save that pleasure until later in the day. Either step down and follow the shore at low tide, or turn left and right to pass the hotel, then turn right down a grassy track to the shore. You can link a scanty series of paths and cross some low rocky headlands. Go through three gates around the head of the harbour, aiming towards Cromwell's Fort, which is the star-shaped fort at the harbour mouth **(30mins)**.

    Cromwell's Fort actually stands on the tiny Port Island, which is separated from Inishbofin by a narrow tidal channel. You can only reach the island dry-shod when the tide is out.

2. Turn round the headland and pick your way along the rugged southern coast of Inishbofin. Stay well above the rocky shore, walking on slopes of grass or heather. There are good views across the sea to Mweelrea and the Twelve Bens. You have to cross a couple of fences and watch out for two deep and rocky chasms that appear quite suddenly. Pass these by climbing round the top of them. A stony track later leads down to a sandy bay **(1hr 15mins)**.

    Note the rugged little island of Inishlyon. It is linked to Inishbofin by a rocky bar at low tide. Views from the sandy bay now extend beyond Mweelrea and include Croagh Patrick, the Nephin Beg Range, and the neighbouring islands of Inishturk and Clare Island.

3. Follow a sandy track inland from the bay and link with a narrow tarmac road. If you want to visit St. Colman's Abbey, then turn left, otherwise walk straight onwards to follow the coast around East End Bay. There is a straggly line of low, whitewashed houses curving round the bay. When the road turns inland, walk down

onto the beach to continue. Aim for a solitary white cottage and come ashore to follow a grassy track uphill alongside it. You pass a gate at a higher level, then follow a boundary wall further uphill and round to the right. When you reach the rocky coast, turn left to follow it, taking in rugged headlands and coves **(2hrs)**.

4. Keep well above the shore and walk along the cliffs on the northern side of the island. Watch out for a rock arch below, known as The Prison, where priests were held captive until 1660. Admire the cliff coast, rocky stacks, and the deeply cut inlet of Ardlea Cove. Cross a fence at the head of Bunnamullen Bay **(3hrs 15mins)**.

5. Walk out of Bunnamullen Bay and turn around the next headland, which has a rocky islet offshore. The cliff coast leads round to the next bay to reach North Beach, where you go through a gate and crunch across a pebbly bar **(4hrs)**.

The pebbly bar forms a natural dam keeping the sea and Lough Bofin apart. Lough Bofin is the largest expanse of fresh water on the island and it attracts a variety of swans, ducks and waders.

At this point you may wish to break for lunch, and the time allowance includes an hour at this point. You might also wish to follow a narrow road across the island at this point, and break at the Doonmore Hotel for food and drink. This road is also available as a short-cut if you find you're running short of time and have to catch your ferry back to Cleggan. It would mean missing out the western end of the island, which is particularly attractive and interesting.

6. Leaving Lough Bofin, continue along a coastal track, passing a few houses, including one rather unusual looking dwelling. You reach another rugged headland where you should keep to the right, towards the coast, but also looking for a large hole in the ground. You can walk down to the bouldery bottom of the hole, and look straight through a long rocky passageway to the open sea. Climb out of the hole and walk towards the sea. You'll find another great gash, and although there is no way down into it, you can cross over it on a natural rock bridge at the far end, marvelling at the size and splendour of the whole thing **(5hrs 30mins)**.

7. Turn left to continue walking along the low cliff coast. The grass is short and bare rock pokes through the ground in places. Pass a bronze memorial cross and climb gradually uphill. From time to time, take a peep over the cliff edge and you'll find the scenery becomes more complex and dramatic as height is gained. You eventually reach a grassy dome surrounded on most sides by cliffs **(6hrs 15mins)**.

The dome, known as Doonmore, is the site of a promontory fort, and you can distinguish its earthen banks on the grassy slope. There is a fine view to the neighbouring island of Inishark. You can see grey stone houses, but they are all in ruins as the island's dwindling and ageing population was finally evacuated.

8. Walking back down the short, steep slope of Doonmore, you'll notice a grassy track running along the southern slopes of the island, in the direction of Bofin Harbour. At first the track is unenclosed; a delightful green ribbon through a landscape of short-cropped grass. Later it becomes a narrow tarmac road passing a number of houses and the Doonmore Hotel. If you want to take a break at the hotel, then allow extra time for it **(7hrs)**.

9. The road twists and turns above the shore as it runs from the Doonmore Hotel back to the pier. There are prominent white navigation towers on the way. If you have completed the full circuit of the island, then doubtless you'll be staying overnight, as you'll probably miss the ferry back to Cleggan. On returning to the pier you can either head to your accommodation or retire to Day's Hotel for your evening meal **(7hrs 30mins)**.

Other walks in the area

As the walk described covers the whole coastline of Inishbofin, there's little left to walk. However, there are some interesting cross-country walks you can make using farm tracks and bog roads.

Places of interest

St. Colman's Abbey, if not visited while walking round the island, should be the subject of a visit some time while you're on the Inishbofin.

Walk 18:
Cleggan, Claddaghduff & Omey Island
Saints and smugglers

Cleggan is a small fishing village with a relatively recent history of smuggling. The surrounding countryside is dotted with archaeological remains that can be studied on a walk to Claddaghduff and back. With a favourable tide you could also include a stroll around the lovely Omey Island, which has a very long history of settlement. Here you will find ancient graveyards, a church buried beneath sand dunes and a 'road' that is washed twice daily by the blue Atlantic.

Grade: Easy

Distance: 17km (10½ miles)

Time: 6 hours (including an hour for lunch)

Start & Finish: Park near the harbour at Cleggan 601584

Map: Ordnance Survey of Ireland Discovery 37

How to get there

> *By car:* Cleggan is signposted from the N59 road north of Clifden. The usual approach to the village is from a road junction in the middle of a broad bog, where half a dozen colourful signs beg you to visit. Park near the harbour.
>
> *By bus:* Michael Nee's Bus runs daily between Clifden and Cleggan, linking with the ferry service to and from Inishbofin. Bus Éireann table number 422 serves Cleggan and Claddaghduff on Wednesdays.

Necessities: Local tide times if you plan to visit Omey Island; **bus timetables** if you are using the limited bus services; **strong shoes** will do instead of boots; **waterproofs** if there is a forecast of rain; **money** for a drink or lunch at Sweeney's Bar & Restaurant at Claddaghduff.

Notes: This is a relatively easy walk, but you do need to be sure of the tide times if you plan to visit Omey Island. The walk around the island from the 'mainland' is 7km (4½ miles) and on a fine day it is absolutely heavenly to walk on the short green turf and enjoy the wealth of archaeological remains.

Introduction

Cleggan is a lovely little fishing village with a relatively recent history of smuggling. One short street full of old buildings leads down to the tiny harbour and its stout stone walls. The harbour in its present form dates from 1822 and was designed by the engineer Alexander Nimmo. You can wander round and look at the fishing boats, and maybe you'll catch the sudden bustle of activity when the Inishbofin ferry comes and goes. If you want to go to Inishbofin, refer to walk 18.

Our walk heads inland from Cleggan, into a quiet and unfrequented bit of countryside where you'll find a couple of ancient

A Megalithic Tomb seen above the shore at Sellerna Bay

Megalithic tombs and a small lake. The little village of Claddaghduff is loosely clustered around a church, and at this point you have to make a decision. With favourable tides, you can go down to Omey Strand and follow the 'road' across to Omey Island. If the tides aren't working to your advantage, then either head back to Cleggan or retire to Sweeney's for lunch and a drink. Maybe afterwards the tide will have ebbed.

Few people were aware of the charms of Omey Island until Ireland's renowned archaeologist Michael Gibbons started taking people there from Clifden. Now a steady stream of people from all over the world enquire about the state of the tides throughout the summer, intent on discovering this gem of an island for themselves. Omey is associated with St. Feichin, who founded a small monastic community there in 7th century. He is the patron saint of the island. There are ancient burial sites on Omey, as well as an ancient church and a village site buried in the sand dunes. Exploring Omey is fascinating, but also time-consuming, and you have to bear in mind the ebb and flow of the tides.

The walk from Claddaghduff back to Cleggan is as easy as the outward leg. It takes in quiet roads and tracks and wanders along a cobbly beach for a while. There is a chance to visit a particularly fine Megalithic tomb before heading back inland to Cleggan. If you are looking for somewhere to eat with an authentic flavour of the area, then try Oliver's Seafood Bar just above the harbour.

The Walk

Assuming you park somewhere near the harbour at Cleggan, simply wander back up through the village along its single street. You can look at all the shops and bars along the street, as you head that way to leave the village.

1. Walk through the village of Cleggan as if following the road back towards Clifden. Pass Joyce's Bar, but turn right before reaching Newman's Bar. A narrow tarmac road gives way to a rough and stony track climbing gently uphill, and there are views back down on Cleggan and Cleggan Bay **(10mins)**.

2. When the rough track reaches a road bend, either continue straight on, or make a detour left through a gate and walk a short way up a track. Just to the right of the track is a collapsed Megalithic tomb. If this is visited, return to the road afterwards to continue **(20mins)**.

3. Follow the road past a house, noting the fuchsia hedgerows alongside that provide a blaze of colour in summer. The road runs down through a crossroads, then climbs to reveal fine views to the left over Courhoor Lough. Look for a small island near the far shore, which is a 'crannóg' **(30mins)**.

   A crannóg is a small island fomerly fortified with a palisade and inhabited by a small group of people, possibly an extended family organised for mutual defence. While some small islands naturally appealed to settlers, in some instances islands could be extended or even built from scratch as crannógs.

4. The road drifts away from Courhoor Lough as it rises, then descends towards Claddaghduff Church. Turn left downhill beside the church to reach Claddaghduff Quay, where the narrow tarmac road simply peters out onto Omey Strand. There may be upturned 'currachs' here, those long, narrow, black-skinned boats that are used on these Atlantic shores **(1hr 15mins)**.

   You need to be absolutely sure of the tide times if you are visiting Omey Island. When the tide is receding, you may find you can paddle ankle-deep across to the island, but don't risk paddling across if the tide is advancing. If Omey Strand is completely clear of water, you should notice wheel marks across the sand, as well as directional 'road' signs pointing out the line of approach for motorists.

5. Follow the marker posts indicating the 'road' across Omey Strand. Once you're about halfway across, you can drift slightly to the right of the posts and aim for a prominent graveyard on the north-eastern corner of the island. Walk mainly along the sandy or rocky shore around the northern side of Omey Island. Be careful when walking on seaweed covered rocks **(1hr 30mins)**.

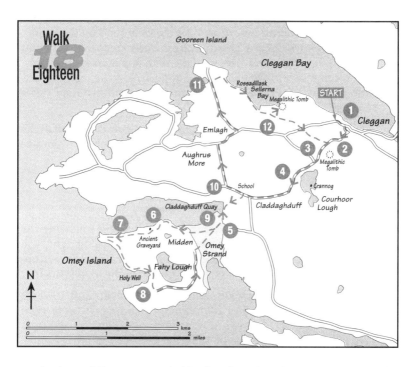

Look carefully at any eroded banks of sand, and you may distinguish darkened layers containing burnt stones, shells and bone fragments. These are ancient 'midden' sites, or the rubbish dumps of the earliest of Omey's coastal dwellers.

6. Further along the shore, climb to the top of a flat-topped grassy knoll known as Cnocán na mBán. Traditionally, this has been held to be a burial place for women, and rabbits burrowing into the hill unearth fragments of human bones. Still further along the shore an eroded sandbank reveals crumbling stone masonry; the remains of a settlement that was occupied from late Medieval times to the late 18th century. Fragments of pottery and clay pipes may be seen on the shore **(2hrs)**.

    Look a short way inland from the old village site to locate the ruins of Teampall Feichin; a church which has been excavated from a deep sand dune. The foundation may date from the 7th century, but the main structure is Medieval. It may have been built in a hollow, before being overwhelmed by drifting sands.

7. Keep walking on lovely, short, green turf speckled with daisies, to the very westernmost point of Omey Island, then turn round the rocky point and walk back towards a rugged little bay. On the way, look out for a tiny Holy Well dedicated to St. Feichin (2hrs 30mins).

8. Head inland from the bay to pick up the only road on the island. There are views of Fahy Lough; a freshwater pool that occupies the middle of the island. The road passes a few houses and fields, then drops down to Omey Strand. Simply follow the marker posts back across the strand to return to Claddaghduff Quay **(3hrs 15mins)**.

9. Follow the road uphill away from Omey Strand and turn left at the church to reach Sweeney's Bar & Restaurant, which incorporates the Claddaghduff Post Office **(3 hr 30mins)**.

    If you want to take a break here for food and drink, then the overall time allowance includes one hour.

10. The road junction beside Sweeney's Bar & Restaurant is signposted for the Dún an Óir Farmhouse B&B. After following the road across a rise of bogland, descending and turning right, you then turn left along another road signposted for Rossadilisk. Continue almost to a huddle of houses at the end of the road **(5hrs)**.

11. Turn right before the houses, and follow a gravel track towards another scattered handful of buildings. The track turns right above the rocky shore, and a narrow path continues. You will later have to walk on the sands of Sellerna Bay. As you cross a small stream spilling into the bay, you can spot a 'cillín', or children's burial ground, marked only by a rash of stones on a slope of grass.

    'Cillín' translates as 'little church' and there are hundreds of these sad little sites scattered across the face of Ireland. Most cillíns were quiet field corners where stillborn and unbaptised babies who died were buried, as they couldn't be buried in consecrated ground. Every little stone you see has a baby buried beneath. Some cillíns were used for the burial of adults during the Great Famine around 1845.

    On the far side of the sandy bay, a Megalithic tomb can be seen on another grassy slope. This can be approached and inspected, but you will have to retrace steps afterwards to leave the bay at a point marked by a solitary lifebelt **(5hrs 30mins)**.

12. A broad track rises inland from a small car park above Sellerna Bay. Follow it uphill and through a crossroads, then continue rising gently along a tarmac road to reach a bend. This bend was encountered earlier in the day's walk, and a left turn leads along a stony track. The track leads over a rise and down to Joyce's Bar, where a left turn leads straight back into Cleggan. If you are hungry, then head for Oliver's Seafood Bar on the way towards the harbour *(6hrs)*.

Other walks in the area

There is an interesting walk on the other side of Cleggan Bay, leading to Cleggan Head, and the area inland has some wonderful Bronze Age standing stones and other features of archaeological interest.

Places of interest

The nearby town of Clifden, the 'Capital of Connemara', is worth visiting. It was a planned town, dating from the early 19th century. Dun Gibbons Inn and the Connemara Walking Centre are places walkers should head for.

Walk 19:
Connemara National Park
Into the wilderness

The Connemara National Park is really quite small and you could make a decent exploration of it in a day. However, you'll also find it is very rugged terrain, with plenty of tussocky bog in the lower parts and steep, rocky slopes as you climb higher. A horseshoe walk around Gleann Mhór takes in the highest mountains around the national park, but be warned that it is a rough and tough walk. You need to be especially careful on Muckanaght as the slopes are very steep and slippery, but there is a way you can avoid the worst parts. On a clear day, with time on your side, it is a wonderful mountain walk.

Grade: Strenuous

Distance: 16km (10 miles)

Time: 7 hours (including an hour for lunch)

Start & Finish: Kylemore Abbey car park 747583

Maps: Ordnance Survey of Ireland Discovery 37 and Harveys Superwalker Map of Connemara

How to get there

> By car: Kylemore Abbey is one of the most prominent places on the main N59 road through the mountains of Connemara between Clifden and Leenane. It is about the only place you can park a car near the start of this walk. It is well worth exploring the Abbey and its grounds while you're in the area.
>
> By bus: Bus Éireann table number 419 links Kylemore with Clifden and Galway on Tuesdays and Saturdays. Table number 61 links Kylemore with Clifden and Westport daily in the summer only. Michael Nee's Bus also serves Kylemore from Clifden in the summer months.

Necessities: Boots as the ground is rugged underfoot; **waterproofs** as the mountains are exposed in rain; **food and drink** as there is nothing in the mountains; **bus timetables** if you're relying on the rather sparse services; **money** in case you're back in time to visit the restaurant at Kylemore Abbey.

Notes: Be warned at the outset that this is a rough and tough horseshoe walk. The terrain is steep and rocky in most parts and bleak and boggy in others. Careful navigation is required in mist and the route is not recommended in bad weather.

Introduction

The walk around the Gleann Mhór Horseshoe takes most of the day to complete, and there are other attractions that demand at least a share of your time. Kylemore Abbey and the Connemara National Park Visitor Centre both lie just off the main N59 road near Letterfrack. Kylemore Abbey has long been admired, while the Connemara National Park is a relatively recent creation. Practically the whole of the walk around the Gleann Mhór Horseshoe is within the National Park, but it is more difficult to complete the walk from the Visitor Centre.

James and Mary Ellis arrived in Letterfrack in 1849, in the aftermath of the Great Famine. They bought land and embarked on building projects that included a meeting house, school, temperance hotel, cottages, dispensary, shop and courthouse. Employment was provided for local people in building, farming, draining the bog and planting trees. James Ellis suffered ill health and the enterprise came to an end in 1857. The Christian Brothers bought the estate and opened an 'Industrial School' in Letterfrack in 1887. This was the largest building in the village, housing over a hundred boys. The place operated until 1974, then most of

Kylemore Abbey is seen on a wooded slope near the start

the land was purchased in 1976 to be developed as the Connemara National Park.

Kylemore Abbey was built by the wealthy Manchester merchant Mitchell Henry for his wife Margaret. They took their honeymoon in Kylemore in 1850 and bought an extensive area of land there in 1862. Work on the site commenced in 1864, with the foundations being laid in 1867. The estate boasted gardens and glasshouses capable of growing bananas, grapes and melons. There was a model farm, stables and cottages. The estate was purchased for the Duke and Duchess of Manchester in 1903, but was sold again in 1920 to the Irish Benedictine nuns. It is now an International Girls' Boarding School, and one of the most important tourist attractions in the west of Ireland. The grounds are especially attractive and offer short scenic walks.

The Walk

Park at Kylemore Abbey and make a note of the opening hours, just in case you're able to fit in a visit later in the day. There is a restaurant on site and you might like to check whether it will be open when you return hungry and thirsty.

1. Leave Kylemore Abbey car park and turn left to follow the main N59 road until it bends left. On the right you'll see a gate flanked by stout iron gateposts, and a track flanked by alder trees leads to a limekiln **(15mins)**.

    Take a look at the limekiln, which has been very well restored. There is a quarry cut into a band of limestone on the lower slopes of Mweelin, which was used to feed the kiln. The lime was used for building work and to reduce the acidity of the soil around Kylemore.

2. Follow a track off to the right, away from the limekiln. There is a gateway in a deer fence, but you don't go through it. Instead, stay on the track, cross a river and follow a prominent drainage ditch across a broad and boggy area. Cross over this channel near a ruined building and continue along a track through rhododendron scrub near Kylemore Farm. The track swings left and you cross a metal step stile over a deer fence. Follow a path upstream beside the Polladirk River to reach a footbridge. Don't cross the footbridge, but walk a little further upstream and cross another little metal footbridge on the left side of the river **(45mins)**.

3. The ascent starts in earnest as you climb straight up a slope of tussocky grass. There is a bit of a level stance, then you climb more steeply all the way to the top of Knockbrack. It is best to outflank any rocky outcrops as the grass gives way to heather. The gradient is severe, but it eases towards the top. There are rock outcrops near the summit, which rises to 442m (1,460ft) and bears a cairn **(1hr 15mins)**.

4. Walk along the broad crest of Knockbrack and cross a gap. Climb up to a tall deer fence, which you should cross with care. Continue uphill and pass a curiously contorted outcrop of rock. When you reach the rocky, hummocky top of Benbrack, there are a number of cairns and the highest one stands at 582m (1,922ft) on a rocky hump **(2hrs)**.

5. Pick a way down a series of little rocksteps to reach the next gap, then pause for a while and study the steep slopes of Muckanaght rising to the south. The slopes are not only steep, but break up into greasy outcrops of rock. The direct ascent is not for the faint-hearted and you should never climb this slope in wet weather.

    One of the reasons why Muckanaght is so steep and slippery is

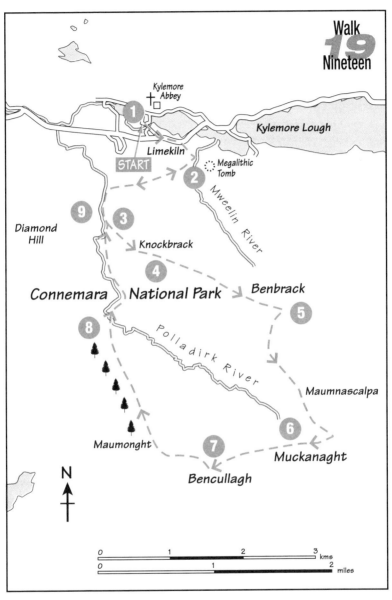

Kylemore Abbey

Kylemore Lough

Limekiln

START

Megalithic Tomb

Mweelin River

Diamond Hill

Knockbrack

Connemara National Park

Benbrack

Polladirk River

Maumnascalpa

Maumonght

Muckanaght

Bencullagh

N

because it is made of schist, rather than the quartzite that makes up most of the Twelve Bens. The schist breaks down to form a finer soil than quartzite, and Muckanaght is able to support an interesting range of flora. This includes mountain sorrel, mountain willow, Alpine saw-wort, Alpine meadow-rue and purple saxifrage.

To proceed in safety, cut off to the left of the gap, climbing diagonally up to another gap to the east of Muckanaght. There is a narrow path which is free of obstacles, and when you reach the higher gap you can swing to the right and climb up a steep and grassy slope to reach the summit of the mountain. There is a slight break of slope halfway up the slope, otherwise you just keep climbing. There are a couple of cairns on the grassy crest and the furthest, rising to 654m (2,153ft), is the highest **(3hrs)**.

This is a fine place to study the extensive view, which is mountainous in most directions. Looking out towards the sea you can spot Tully Mountain, while closer to hand is Diamond Hill. Looking far beyond Benbrack and Benchoona you see the lofty peak of Mweelrea. The Sheeffry Hills and Ben Gorm are alongside, followed by Leenane Hill and the Devilsmother. The Maum Turk Mountains and the highest of the Twelve Bens are in view, including the towering Benbaun. Errisbeg is more distantly in view. The next summit in line on this walk is Bencullagh.

As you're on the highest part of the horseshoe walk, and can enjoy extensive views in fine weather, this makes a good place to break for lunch. The time allowance given for the walk assumes you'll spend an hour on the summit.

6. Descend from Muckanaght on a steep slope of grass to reach a gap covered in blanket bog. Climb uphill on short grass, heather and moss, which is peppered with stones, then swing left near the top. You'll reach a cairn at 632m (2,084ft) on the summit of Bencullagh **(4hrs 30mins)**.

7. Although Bencullagh is the last summit on the round, there's quite a long walk-out to complete the circuit. Walk down a heathery slope that becomes rockier towards the next gap. There is a ridge with a couple of rocky humps bearing cairns, then there is quite a steep descent. Heather, grass and broken rock are crossed on the way down to a tall deer fence on the lower slopes **(5hrs 15mins)**.

8. Cross the fence with care and turn left to follow it across the boggy floor of Gleann Mhór. There are some vague paths trodden across the bog towards the Polladirk River, and you should cross the river at a shallow point before it plunges into a deep gorge. Pick your way across the steep slopes of Knockbrack, staying high above the river and following a rugged terrace across the flank of the mountain. Look ahead and you'll spot the footbridge spanning the Polladirk River, which you passed earlier in the day. Aim for this bridge, but don't cross it **(6hrs 15mins)**.

9. All you need to do to bring the walk to a close it retrace your earlier steps of the day's walk. Follow the path downstream, crossing the metal step stile and walking through rhododendrons to reach the drainage channel. Cross the channel and follow the track alongside it, crossing a river to return to the limekiln. A track from

the limekiln leads back to the main N59 road, where you turn left to return to Kylemore Abbey (**7hrs**).

If the restaurant at Kylemore Abbey is still open, you may wish to retire there for a hearty meal. You may not have enough time to explore the Abbey and its wonderful grounds, but you can pick up some information and enjoy some easier strolling around the area another day.

Other walks in the area

The Twelve Bens offer some rough and tough walks for people who like their mountains rugged. Kylemore Abbey offers a lovely, easy, lakeside walk where you can admire splendid trees along the shore.

Places of interest

Kylemore Abbey, the Gothic Church and the Victorian Walled Garden are places that could take all day to explore properly. The Connemara National Park Visitor Centre is reached from the village of Letterfrack.

Walk 20:
The Glencorbet Horseshoe
A bite of the Bens

A walk around the Glencorbet Horseshoe is one of the most entertaining ways to explore the Twelve Bens and climb Benbaun. The route is perhaps a little easier than some of the other horseshoe walks in the Twelve Bens, and certainly it cannot be any more difficult. The circuit allows you to enjoy fine views over Kylemore Lough, as well as enjoying the panorama from Benbaun, the highest mountain in the range.

Grade: Strenuous

Distance: 15km (9½ miles)

Time: 6 hours (including an hour for lunch)

Start & Finish: Glencorbet 800574

Maps: Ordnance Survey of Ireland Discovery 37 and Harveys Superwalker Map of Connemara

How to get there

> *By car:* The main N59 road between Clifden and Leenane passes Kylemore and reaches the Pass Inn Hotel. The R344 road through the Inagh Valley to Recess can be followed through a forest, then the first turning to the right is for Glencorbet. It is important to park off this road, maybe beside a bridge, or with permission further along near some houses, but you must not block any access point.
>
> *By bus:* Bus Éireann table number 61 between Westport and Clifden passes the Pass Inn Hotel on the main N59 road in summer. The only other service is the occasional table number 419 service between Clifden and Galway on Tuesday and Saturday.

Necessities: Boots as the mountains are rocky and boggy; **waterproofs** as there is little shelter from rain; **food and drink** as there is nothing along the way; **compass** to take bearings in mist.

Notes: The walk around the Glencorbet Horseshoe is quite tough, but can be accomplished by most fit hill walkers with no problems. Muckanaght rises at the head of the glen and is avoided on this particular walk. A direct ascent needs special care as the slopes are very steep and can be slippery when wet. The walk is not recommended in mist, but could be completed well enough by using a compass.

Introduction

The Twelve Bens of Connemara form a fine range of mountains. Proud, bright summits of quartzite raise their heads high above brown, boggy glens. The main summits are arranged in a roughly cruciform shape, though the ridges connect awkwardly in the middle, leaving the deep gap of Maumina to be confronted by anyone trying to walk all the way across the range. Between the ridges are broad and boggy glens; a couple of them planted with forests, and a couple more featuring small farmsteads. The mountains around each glen make fine horseshoe walks, of which the Glencorbet Horseshoe is just one. You can refer to walk 20 for details of the Gleann Mhór Horseshoe and walk 21 for the classic Glencoaghan Horseshoe.

The name Glencorbet has been translated as the 'valley of the chariots' and the 'valley of the boulders'. The latter seems more appropriate as there are indeed slopes of boulders in many places, mostly glacial rubble, but also some that have simply fallen from broken cliffs. The head of the valley is dominated by Muckanaght, which has very steep slopes. While it is the true head of the horseshoe walk, it is actually avoided on this walk in favour of a route cutting across its slopes. Muckanaght is not a place to visit in wet weather as the slopes can be treacherously slippery.

A walker on the rugged slopes of Benbaun above Glencorbet

The walk climbs gradually from Glencorbet and takes in the little summit of Maolin first. There are splendid views overlooking Kylemore Lough and Kylemore Abbey, which prove to be amazingly colourful in good weather. After crossing the rugged, hummocky crest of Benbrack you see the steep slopes of Muckanaght rising impressively ahead. On this walk you can cut across from one gap to another, avoiding the high parts of the mountain completely. The steep slopes of Benfree give way to the stony slopes of Benbaun, which is the highest of the Twelve Bens. A stony slope and a broad and boggy crest lead to Knockpasheemore, from where you can descend into Glencorbet to complete the round.

Lovely, green, grassy fields, in contrast to the brown bogs and rocky slopes beyond surround the little farmsteads in Glencorbet. Farmers have exploited bands of limestone on the floor of the glen, clearing the rubble and nurturing the soil to establish an oasis of high fertility in an otherwise poor landscape suitable only for rough grazing.

The Walk

Remember, if you take a car along the road into Glencorbet, to park it very neatly in an obviously convenient space, or obtain permission to park. Either way, be sure not to cause any kind of obstruction.

1. The narrow tarmac access road into Glencorbet crosses a bridge over the Kylemore River. You'll see that the bridge was founded on a limestone outcrop. There are only a handful of buildings ahead, and when the tarmac ends there is a stony track heading off to the left. Follow the track for a short way, then leave it to start climbing uphill **(15mins)**.

2. The slope is fairly gentle, and there are tilted blocks of quartzite on the slope, with stones lying scattered over the grassy patches. At a higher level the ground is wetter and the scattering of stones continues. A little limestone hill is crossed, which is distinguished by having a cover of short, green grass in contrast to the longer moorland grass elsewhere on the slopes **(30mins)**.

3. Cross a junction of fences in a dip and continue up a rough and boggy crest of grass and heather. The crest is quite hummocky but generally you'll find that the trend is uphill. There is a short, steep, rocky slope leading down to a boggy gap, then a steep, grassy ascent onto Maolan. There is a small cairn at 477m (1,577ft) on the summit **(1hr 15mins)**.

    Spend a while scouting around the summit area, as there are spectacular views over Kylemore Lough and Kylemore Abbey. The slopes of Maolan fall away steeply, so that there is a great sense of depth to the view.

4. You'll see the end of a fence near the summit cairn on Maolan. Go round it and follow the fence down a short, steep slope to cross a boggy gap. Climb uphill and drift away from the fence to follow a rough and rocky ridge. It is easier to walk up this ridge than it looks at first sight. There is a fairly good path and the rock outcrops are almost like a stairway. When you reach the rocky, hummocky top of Benbrack, there are a number of cairns and the highest on stands at 582m (1,922ft) on a rocky hump **(1hr 45mins)**.

5. Pick a way down a series of little rocksteps to reach the next gap, then pause for a while and study the steep slopes of Muckanaght rising to the south. The slopes are not only steep, but break up into greasy outcrops of rock. The direct ascent is not for the faint-hearted and you should never climb this slope in wet weather.

    One of the reasons why Muckanaght is so steep and slippery is because it is made of schist, rather than the quartzite that makes up most of the Twelve Bens. The schist breaks down to form a finer

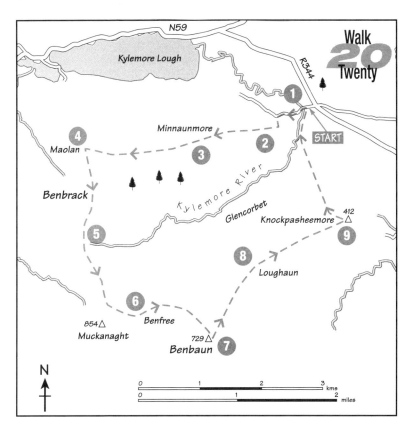

soil than quartzite, and Muckanaght is able to support an interesting range of flora. This includes mountain sorrel, mountain willow, Alpine saw-wort, Alpine meadow-rue and purple saxifrage.

To proceed in safety, cut off to the left of the gap, climbing diagonally up to another gap to the east of Muckanaght. There is a narrow path which is free of obstacles, leading you up to a higher gap **(2hrs 30mins)**.

6. Climb steeply north-east from the gap, up a grassy slope that is peppered with stones in places. There is a slight break of slope, otherwise the ascent is unremitting. There is a cairn on the grassy summit of Benfree at 638m (2,095ft). There is a short, steep, grassy descent from Benfree, then the terrain changes markedly to a broken, stony, rocky ridge leading up to Benbaun. There is a vague trodden path passing a few grassy patches, but most of the way is on rock, where the broken quartzite crunches underfoot. The summit of Benbaun rises to 729m (2,395ft) and bears a trig point **(3hrs 15mins)**.

Even in this harsh rocky terrain you can find little tufts of vegetation surviving. Look carefully for little cushions of thrift, clubmosses and tiny St. Patrick's cabbages.

The view is remarkably extensive, taking in the lake-strewn Roundstone Bog, Cregg Hill and its TV masts, followed by Bencullagh, Muckanaght, Benfree and Diamond Hill. Tully Mountain is near the sea, then Knockbrack, Benbrack and Maolan lead the eye to Doughruagh and Benchoona. Across Killary Harbour you can see Mweelrea, the Sheeffry Hills and Ben Gorm. Leenane Hill and the Devilsmother are seen, as well as the central parts of the Maum Turk Mountains. Bencorr, Bencollaghduff, Derryclare, Benbreen and Benglenisky lead the eye round full circle through the Twelve Bens.

If you're blessed with a clear day you might like to break for lunch on the summit of Benbaun. The time allowance for the walk assumes you'll spend an hour on top, though in bad weather you might break early on a lower gap.

7. To descend from Benbaun you should first walk roughly north-wards across the stony crest of the mountain, then locate a stony path that drops from one rocky slab to another. Even if you don't locate the path, it is easy enough to walk down the slabs as they're pitched at a reasonable angle. Swing to the right as you descend and the rocky flank of Benbaun gives way to a stony, hummocky area, which in turn gives way to a broad, hummocky crest of blanket bog **(4hrs 45mins)**.

8. Walk along the broad crest, following a vague path passing only occasional outcrops of rock. There are fine views along the Inagh Valley and towards the Maum Turk Mountains. Keep to this crest to reach a rocky end called Knockpasheemore, which rises slightly to 412m (1,362ft) and bears a cairn **(5hrs 15mins)**.

9. Retrace steps slightly from the summit of Knockpasheemore, then drop down into Glencorbet. There are rocky areas on the slope of bog and grass, and halfway down there are some steep slabs that you should avoid. Aim for the bridge crossing the Kylemore River near the houses, which you crossed at the start of the day's walk. There is a broad and wet bogland to cross, but there is a firm footing available beside the river. You pass an old bridge before you reach the tarmac farm road at the next bridge to end the walk.

Other walks in the area
While Glencorbet is part of the rugged range called the Twelve Bens, it also faces the northern end of the Maum Turk Mountains, where there are even more opportunities to walk well off the beaten track.

Places of interest
You're not too far from Kylemore Abbey if you haven't visited the place while enjoying other walks in the area.

Walk 21:
The Glencoaghan Horseshoe
A mountain classic

The Glencoaghan Horseshoe is one of the classic mountain walks in Connacht. It is a tough undertaking, as most of the way you'll be walking on bare and broken rock. One or two sections call for scrambling skills and there are plenty of steep ascents and descents. There is a youth hostel at the foot of Benlettery and most people start the walk from that point. Curiously, each mountain climbed is progressively higher in turn until you reach Bencorr, then the last one on the round, which is Derryclare, is lower. Make no mistake, this is an arduous walk that takes all day and you need to tread with care at all times.

Grade: Strenuous

Distance: 16km (10 miles)

Time: 7½ hours (including an hour for lunch)

Start & Finish: Benlettery Youth Hostel 777483

Maps: Ordnance Survey of Ireland Discovery 37 & 44 and Harveys Superwalker Map of Connemara

How to get there
> *By car:* Benlettery Youth Hostel is on the main N59 road between Clifden and Recess. Cars can be parked on a short loop of old road just to the east of the hostel, taking care not to block any access points.
> *By bus:* Bus Éireann table number 419 occasionally passes Benlettery Youth Hostel. Michael Nee's Bus runs from Clifden to Galway and passes the hostel every day.

Necessities: Boots as the mountains are rocky underfoot; **waterproofs** as there is little shelter from rain; **food and drink** as there is nothing on the way; **compass** to take bearings in mist.

Notes: This is a classic mountain walk, but remember that it is also a rough and rocky circuit where you'll have to scramble on bare rock in a couple of places. It is not a walk you should choose in bad weather, and if you decide to cut the walk short you need to be careful when you choose your escape route. In clear weather, with time on your side, it is a most enjoyable and exciting walk.

Introduction

Glencoaghan is a deeply-cut glacial valley surrounded by steep-sided, rocky mountains. The mountains are mostly composed of bright quartzite, which forms sheer cliffs in places and breaks up into angular boulders and scree slopes. Vegetation cover is sparse, consisting of little rugs of heather and grass on the ridges, with blanket bog in the floor of the glen. In places where grazing sheep cannot reach, you can find plants such as bilberry, crowberry, thrift and St. Patrick's cabbage. In some parts there is a ground-hugging dwarf variety of juniper.

Walkers descend rocky slopes to a gap at the head of Glencoaghan

The historian Roderick O'Flaherty penned some of the first topographical descriptions of these mountains. He singled out Benlettery for special mention, though he knew it as 'Bindowglass', ascribing it a phenomenal height: *'On the north-west of Balynahinsy are the twelve high mountains of Bennabeola, called by marriers the twelve stakes, being the first land they discover as they come from the maine. Bindowglass is the highest of them, and, next the lake, is two miles high; and hath standing water on the top of it, wherein they say if any washeth his head, he becomes hoare.'*

It is advisable to choose a clear day for this walk, with a favourable weather forecast. There is a steep climb at the outset, followed by a fairly straightforward ridge walk. However, you reach a gap between Bengower and Benbreen where you have to scramble down a steep and rocky slope, then climb up a steep slope of scree. You'll lose a lot of time in this sort of terrain, and as the walk progresses the next gap is even lower, and the mountains ahead are even higher. Even when you've crossed the final summit, there's quite a long and steep descent to the road, and that can be hard on the knees at the end of the day.

Throughout the day you have to keep an eye on the map, measuring your progress against the clock, ready to resort to compass bearings if the cloud descends, and making quite sure that you're off the mountains before nightfall. It is an exciting mountain walk, but it has to be treated with respect too.

Walk 21: Walking on the bare and rocky slopes of Bencollaghduff

Walk 23: Looking along the length of Lough Coolin to the outflow

Walk 24: Walking across bare limestone pavement near Gort na gCapall

Walk 25: A Japanese walker leads the way to the top of Raheen Barr

The Walk

Walkers who choose to stay at Benlettery Youth Hostel can walk out of the door and start climbing immediately. If you arrive by car, then park on a loop of old road to the east of the hostel.

1. Walk up the hostel driveway and head off to the left of the building. Cross a stile over a fence and walk straight uphill passing a few trees. Cross another fence on the lower slopes of Benlettery. The direction is straight uphill, with only the vaguest paths on the steep and unremitting slope. Skirt any rock outcrops as you climb, and make zig-zagging manoeuvres to ease the gradient where necessary. If you drift to the left you'll reach a couple of cairns on a high shoulder and there is a path you can follow. If you need an excuse to stop, then turn round and admire the unfolding view. The slope steepens as you climb, but finally eases as you approach the 577m (1,904ft) summit **(1hr)**.

    Look southwards from the summit as the view is amazing. Dozens of little lakes of all shapes and sizes fill the broad, rolling lowlands of Roundstone Bog.

2. A rugged ridge leads from Benlettery to Bengower, but the gradients are relatively easy. Cross the broad, stony, heathery gap, climb uphill past a prominent cairn, then cross another little gap. A gravel path leads up a blocky slope to reach the summit cairn on Bengower at 664m (2,184ft). You should pause here to consider your next move with care **(1hr 30mins)**.

3. As you leave the summit of Bengower, look carefully towards the next gap to spot a cairn on the slope. From that point, follow a trodden path that zig-zags downhill and follow it carefully. There are five rocky places on the steep descent where you'll have to scramble down using your hands. There are plenty of good holds, and you should always look for the next stretch of path below before making your move. There should be no problems getting down if you are agile and have a head for heights, but groups will tend to move slowly at this point **(2hrs)**.

4. It is rather galling to land on the gap and then have to face the steep scree slopes of Benbreen. Most walkers seem to walk up and down a tongue of fine scree, but there is better purchase for your feet on the more bouldery slopes just to the left. It is an arduous ascent and you have to be careful not to send any boulders crashing downhill as you climb. There is a cairn at 691m (2,276ft) on the summit of Benbreen **(2hrs 30mins)**.

    There is a fine view around the Glencoaghan Horseshoe from Benbreen. If you're keeping an eye on the time, you might think that you're going too slow, but in fact this first stretch does take quite a long time. The rest of the walk is undoubtably tough, but you should be able to cover it rather more quickly.

5. The crest of Benbreen is made of rocky humps and bumps. You can walk over them all, or you can keep to the right and outflank them. The crest curves to the right, but be sure you swing to the left when the ground gets steeper. A trodden path of sorts drops down rocky ribs and slabs, then a grassy slope peppered with rocks leads down to a gap **(3hrs)**.

You'll notice that there is a lower gap off to the left, but you don't go down to it. That gap is called Maumina, and is the lowest gap in the Twelve Bens. The bulky mountain rising beyond it is Benbaun, which is the highest of the Twelve Bens. You can climb Benbaun with reference to walk 21.

The gap is a good place to break for lunch, as you have most of the hard work accomplished, and there's likely to be more shelter here than on the tops. The time allowance for the walk assumes you'll break on the gap for one hour.

6. Climb straight uphill from the gap on a steep slope of broken rock. The ascent comes in three stages, taking in narrow gravel paths with fairly definite rocky shoulders between them. The last climb is quite rocky and you'll need to use your hands, though there are plenty of holds. The gradient eases and the crest of Bencollaghduff is broad and bouldery. There is a cairn at 696m (2,280ft) on the summit **(4hrs 30mins)**.

Looking westwards, you begin to see the form of the Maum Turk Mountains more clearly than on the first half of the walk.

7. Leaving the summit of Bencollaghduff you start descending quite gently across a slope scattered with boulders. As the slope steepens towards the next gap, there are rocky ribs and slabs to cross, as well as an extensive area of bare quartzite. The gap is like a rock-walled notch that you have to scramble across, but it is filled with a soft strip of blanket bog. There are trodden paths climbing steeply up a rocky slope, leading to a cairn on a rocky shoulder. There is a rock bar and a slab to cross before a steep and bouldery climb leads to the summit of Bencorr. There is a cairn at 711m (2,336ft) and a view to be savoured **(5hrs 30mins)**.

From this airy perch you can see southwards to Cashel Hill and across the lake-spattered Roundstone Bog to Errisbeg. There are close-up views of the Twelve Bens, and beyond Benbaun you can see Doughruagh and Benchoona. Mweelrea, the Sheeffry Hills and Ben Gorm fill the horizon, and most of the Maum Turk Mountains are in view. The next summit in line, Derryclare, can be studied before you head in that direction.

8. Follow a path southwards from Bencorr, on a steep and stony path

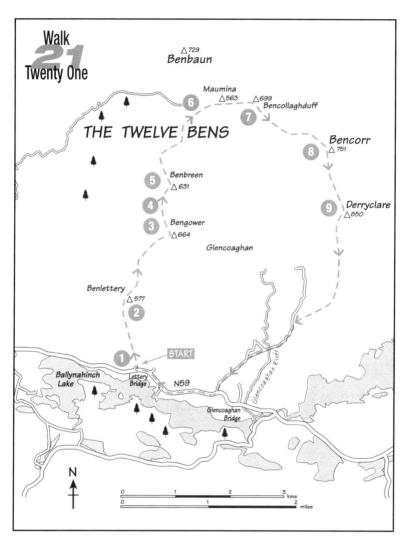

Benbaun
△ 729

Maumina
△ 563
△ 699
Bencollaghduff

THE TWELVE BENS

6

7

Bencorr
△ 751

8

Benbreen
△ 631

5

4

Derryclare
△850

9

3

Bengower
△664

Glencoaghan

Benlettery
△ 577

2

START

1

Ballynahinch
Lake

Lettery
Bridge

N59

Glencoaghan River

Glencoaghan
Bridge

N

0   1   2   3 kms
0   1   2 miles

at first, with the gradient easing towards a broad gap. You pass a few small drystone shelters before reaching the gap. A gravel path leads uphill, passing interesting outcrops of highly contorted rock. The summit of Derryclare is bare rock, rising to 675m (2,220ft), crowned with a cairn **(6hrs 15mins)**.

Take a last good look around at the view before commencing the descent. The way down is steep and rugged in places and you'd be better to watch where you are planting your feet.

9.   Leave the summit of Derryclare and continue walking south-wards. There is a trodden path on the higher stony slopes, leading

onto heathery slopes below. Keep looking to the right until you have a clear view of the minor road in Glencoaghan far below. Pick a way down to this road, avoiding rocky outcrops, then turn left to follow it out of the glen. The road crosses the Glencoaghan River, twisting and turning and eventually joining the main N59 road. Turn right to follow the road alongside Ballynahinch Lake to return to Benlettery Youth Hostel **(7hrs 30mins)**.

Other walks in the area

The Twelve Bens offer a handful of fine horseshoe walks, but it is also possible to enjoy some low-level walking around the base of the mountains, or in nearby forests. Roundstone Bog and Errisbeg Mountain to the south offer some wonderful walking in good weather.

Places of interest

Ballynahinch Castle Hotel is a fine place to stay on the southern side of Ballynahinch Lake. If you follow the main road in the direction of Clifden, you can visit the Connemara History & Heritage Centre.

Walk 22:
Máméan & the Maum Turk Mountains
A blessing for Connemara

They say that St. Patrick never set foot in Connemara, but instead he climbed to the gap of Máméan in the Maum Turk Mountains and gave the rugged countryside beyond his blessing from afar. Máméan is the subject of an annual pilgrimage and scattered across the gap you'll find holy wells, Stations of the Cross, a statue of St. Patrick, a little chapel and altar, and a hollow known as St. Patrick's Bed. Rising above Máméan you'll find a fine stretch of the Maum Turk Mountains, and if you climb Binn Chaonaigh and Binn Idir an Dá Log you may find your appetite is whetted for more challenging walks in these rugged mountains. The lower parts of the walk are part of the waymarked Western Way.

Grade: Strenuous

Distance: 13km (8 miles)

Time: 5 hours (including an hour for lunch)

Start & Finish: At a car park at the foot of Máméan 892495

Maps: Ordnance Survey of Ireland Discovery 37 & 44 and Harveys Superwalker Map of Connemara

How to get there
    By car: Máméan is signposted from the main N59 road near Recess, as well as from the R344 road near the Lough Inagh Lodge on the road from Kylemore to Recess. Follow the narrow minor road to reach a car park at the foot of the gap. An iron gate above the car park is marked with the name Máméan and there is also a signpost indicating the Western Way.
    By bus: There are no bus services closer than Recess.

Necessities: Boots as the mountains are steep and rocky; **waterproofs** as there is no shelter from the rain; **food and drink** as there is nothing along the way; **compass** as you'll need to take bearings in mist.

Notes: The walk over this part of the Maum Turk Mountains involves following a rugged ridge where you have to change direction several times. In clear weather there should be no problem, but in mist you will need to take compass bearings to connect the summits and gaps correctly. The descent to the gap called Mám Ochóige needs particular care. The low-level parts of the walk are much easier and are part of the waymarked Western Way.

Introduction

The central part of the Maum Turk Mountains is where you'll find the highest mountain in the range. Binn Idir an Dá Log is head and shoulders above the other rugged peaks in the range, and it can be climbed conveniently in association with neighbouring Binn Chaonaigh. The

The Western Way is followed into the mountains at Mámèan

two summits are almost severed from the rest of the range by the low-slung gaps of Mámèan and Mám Ochóige. Both gaps lie on excavated fault lines in the underlying quartzite.

Climbing onto Binn Chaonaigh by way of Mámèan is fairly straightforward, but descending from Binn Idir an Dá Log to Mám Ochóige needs rather more care. Most of the ridge is composed of broken or bare rock, with only little rugs of heather and grass in some parts. The ridge zig-zags back and forth, so in mist it is necessary to keep taking bearings to be sure of hitting the gaps and peaks correctly.

Mámèan is associated with St. Patrick's travels, and according to legend he climbed to the gap and gave the whole of Connemara a blessing, rather than travel any further into the wilderness! The historian Roderick O'Flaherty wrote of the place as follows: '*At Mam-en, there springs out of a stone a litle water, named from St. Patrick, which is a present remedy against murrein in cattel, not only applyed, but alsoe as soon as tis sent for they begin to have ease.*'

There was a traditional pilgrimage to Mámèan, and although it fell out of favour in the past, it was revived in the 1980s. A number of stone structures were erected on the broad and stony gap, and each one bears its name carved in Irish. There is a small chapel called Cillín Phádraig and a covered altar called Carraig Aifrinn Phádraig Naofa. Note the Connemara Marble on the altar, and the lovely collection of ferns growing behind. St. Patrick's Bed, or Leaba Phádraig, is a hollow in the rock. You can find St. Patrick's Well, or Tobar Phádraig, and St. Patrick's Source Well, or Buntobar Phádraig Naofa, which was dedicated in recent years. There is a statue of St. Patrick inscribed Pádraig Mór na hÉireann, which was flown in by helicopter. The Stations of the Cross surround the site in a wide circuit.

The Walk

Follow the signposts for Mámeán and park at the car park at the foot of the gap. The road leading away from the car park, signposted as the Western Way, will be followed later in the day when you return to this point.

1. Leave the car park and follow a grassy track uphill, crossing a stile beside an iron gate. The gate is marked with the name Mámeán. The track crosses a small stream and runs further uphill. Sometimes the surface is grassy and sometimes it is stony, but it is nearly always flanked by kerbstones and easy to distinguish. Occasional Western Way markers bear yellow arrows pointing uphill. The track runs across bare rock towards the top, and you'll see the Chapel and other structures off to the left (**30mins**).

    Take a good look around all the features on the gap of Mámeán. The oldest structures are St. Patrick's Bed and St. Patrick's Well. The chapel, altar, statue and Stations of the Cross are all quite recent.

2. A fence crosses the broad gap of Mámeán. Turn left and walk uphill alongside it, climbing on a bouldery slope or steep grass. You reach a shoulder of the mountain which is set at an easier angle, then climb uphill on rugged ground again. If you look carefully at dark and damp cracks in the rock, you'll notice wood sorrel and St. Patrick's cabbage grows out of reach of grazing sheep. The fence twists and turns, but remains a good guide if there is mist on the mountain. When the gradient eases on a hummocky slope of decaying blanket bog, the fence drifts off to the right. You should climb directly to the summit of Binn Chaonaigh, and you'll find two cairns; the highest being at 633m (2,076ft) beyond a pool of water (**1hr**).

    In mist you could probably reach the summit of Binn Chaonaigh without a compass, but you should use one to negotiate the rest of the rugged ridge as it does change direction several times and there are only scanty paths to follow. The top of Binn Chaonaigh is a jumble of low rock outcrops, liberally scattered with stones, bearing patches of heather and crowberry.

3. An indistinct path crosses crunchy quartzite gravel and runs down to a gap below Binn Chaonaigh. You also have to cross some bare rock and patches of heather, and it is the same sort of terrain all the way across the rugged gap. Climbing up the next slope, you walk on grass, heather and boulders, and the slope becomes rather rockier as height is gained. The next part of the ridge is hummocky rock, and you have two options to proceed.

    Some walkers like to stay high on the ridge and others like to keep to the left of it. A small cairn sits on a rocky hump on the ridge, then there's a short, steep descent to a little gap (**1hr 45mins**).

4. Walkers generally keep to the left of the next ridge of broken rock, following a clear band of white quartz uphill. There is a summit bearing a cairn just to the right as you reach the top. The rest of the rugged ridge is broad and hummocky, covered in broken rock, stones and heather. A final short, rocky climb passes a prominent streak of quartz before reaching the summit cairn at 702m (2,307ft) on Binn Idir an Dá Log **(2hrs)**.

    Views stretch away across the lowland Roundstone Bog to Cashel Hill, then beyond Ballynahinch Lake your eye roves through the Twelve Bens. You can spot Derryclare, Bengower, Benbreen, Bencorr, Bencollaghduff, Benbaun, Benbrack and Maolan. Doughruagh is seen away beyond Kylemore. Closer to hand are Knocknahillion and Letterbreckaun, then further away are Mweelrea, Ben Gorm, Leenane Hill, the Devilsmother and Maumtrasna's long plateau. Across the Maum Valley lie Bunnacunneen, Lugnabrick and Mount Gable. Looking back along the ridge you can see Binn Chaonaigh.

    If you're on this airy perch on a clear, fine day, then you might like to break for lunch and make the most of the panorama. The time allowance for the walk assumes you'll spend an hour on the summit. In wet and windy weather, with no view in any direction, you might simply grab a bite to eat and keep moving.

5. Walk further along the ridge and you'll pick up a gravelly path leading downhill. Little cushions of thrift grow on scree and broken rock, but later there are boggy patches, grass and heather. Vague paths lead you to a rocky edge overlooking the gap of Mám Ochóige, and you need to take great care on the descent.

    There are a couple of cairns on the rocky edge, and you need to decide whether to outflank the cliffs by walking right or left. Left is easier, but only if the correct line of descent is located. There is a steep, slippery, poorly trodden path, slanting to the left down a small scree gully where the rock actually overhangs. It is an unmistakable route, but you have to look for it carefully. Another steep slope of rock and grass leads down to the left of a rock-bound lough on the gap **(3hrs 30mins)**.

6. The little lough isn't quite sitting on the lowest part of the gap. You have to walk past the rocky rim of the lough, then cross a grassy hump where there's a fence to the right, before descending to the lowest part of the gap. This is full of decaying blanket bog, and you turn left to walk down a steep slope of short grass. There are boulders embedded into the slope, and you walk down into a steep-sided, rock-walled valley between the mountains **(3hrs 45mins)**.

7. Keep to the left side of a tumbling stream, passing little waterfalls where the river mainly runs on a bed of bare rock. Looking across

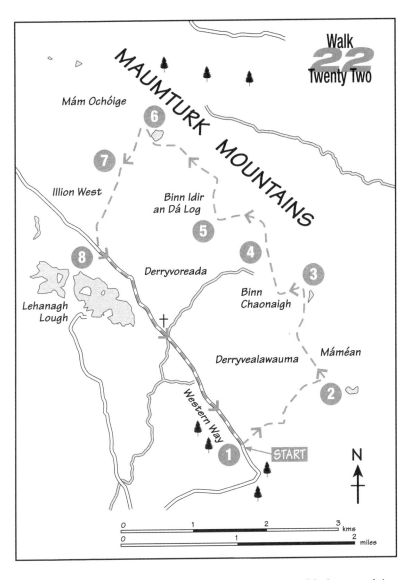

the river you can see old potato ridges; a most unlikely part of the mountain for cultivation, showing how every scrap of land was once pressed into service. At a lower level, drift away from the river to avoid a wide bend, and walk across a boggy area to reach a road bridge **(4hrs)**.

8. Turn left to follow the narrow minor road over a gentle rise, passing a handful of houses, all arranged to the left of the road at Derryvoreada. The road is part of the waymarked Western Way,

rising again to pass a building that was recently used as a chapel, and before that was a National School. Continue along the road, passing more farms and houses, again all arranged to the left, at Derryvealawauma. The road rises gently to return to the car park at the foot of Mámean.

Other walks in the area

The Maum Turk Mountains are rough and tough from end to end. Not only do they offer up to a week's walking, but some walkers like to cover them from end to end in an arduous day's walk. The low-level Western Way offers easier walks in the area, which you can check by obtaining a copy of the Western Way guidebook.

Places of interest

If you're around the tiny, scattered village of Recess, you'll be able to see objects made of Connemara Marble at Joyce's of Recess. The stone is quarried locally, as well as in other parts of Connemara.

Walk 23:
Clonbur & Mount Gable
Joyce Country

Mount Gable is only a hill, but it has the aspect of a mountain. It occupies a strategic position in Joyce Country, between the central plains of Ireland and the great mountain ranges of the west. To the north is Lough Mask, while to the south is Lough Corrib. Views from the summit are wonderfully varied; a reflection of the position of Mount Gable. The ascent can be conveniently started from the village of Clonbur, using a variety of quiet country roads, hill tracks and paths.

Grade: Moderate

Distance: 13km (8 miles)

Time: 5 hours (including an hour for lunch)

Start & Finish: Clonbur 095558

Map: Ordnance Survey of Ireland Discovery 38

How to get there

By car: The village of Clonbur is on a narrow neck of land between Lough Corrib and Lough Mask. The R345 road runs through the village, linking ultimately with the main N59 road at Leenane and the main N84 road at Ballinrobe and Headford. Clonbur is roughly halfway between Galway city and the large town of Westport.

By bus: Bus Éireann table number 420 serves Clonbur daily in the summer, but less frequently at other times of the year. Other services reach the nearby village of Cong.

Necessities: Boots as the slopes and summit of Mount Gable can be boggy; **waterproofs** as the summit is exposed in wet weather; **food and drink** as there is nothing apart from what you find in Clonbur.

Notes: The walk over Mount Gable is fairly straightforward, but you do need to be careful if walking over the summit in mist. There are some good tracks and paths, but some areas are boggy, while others are steep, rugged and pathless.

Introduction

When Thomas Joyce left Wales in the 14th century he settled in Connacht, where his son married an O'Flaherty girl. The Joyce clan was founded, and they acquired a territory that bears their name to this day – Joyce Country. Bounded on the north by Lough Mask and on the south by Lough Corrib, Joyce Country extends westwards into the Maum Valley and embraces a number of little known hills. Mount Gable is one of these hills, though its name seldom appears on maps, and the Ordnance Survey call it Benlevy.

The little village of Clonbur is ideally situated for an ascent of Mount Gable. There are a couple of places to stay and a handful of

133

A view of Lough Coolin from high on Mount Gable

pubs and restaurants if you decide to stay overnight. When you start walking through the countryside you'll find waymark posts have been planted at some of the road junctions and on paths around Lough Coolin, but the route described below only follows the waymarks from time to time. There is a fine old bog road climbing onto Mount Gable and you can descend to Lough Coolin afterwards to link with the waymarked trail.

When the Guinness family held Ashford Castle near Cong, they had their own private carriage ride across country, around Lough Coolin, and back home. It was a remarkable road, crossing bridges over the public highways, rather than using them. There were also screens of trees along some stretches, shielding users of the carriage ride from observing the local peasantry at work. You'll be able to follow part of the route around Lough Coolin, though it has been largely overwhelmed by bog and heather and hasn't been used for over a century.

While Mount Gable isn't a particularly high hill, it does have some steep and rugged slopes, and is quite boggy in places. As the crest is broad and featureless, you should exercise care if you walk over it in mist. If the weather turns out to be against you, it is still worth considering a short walk around Lough Coolin, which is fully waymarked. Most of the time you'll have this area to yourself, but occasionally you'll find groups of youngsters out walking from the nearby Petersburg Outdoor Education Centre. Mount Gable is also visited by geologists on account of the rather complex nature of its bedrock.

The Walk

Park in any convenient space in Clonbur and you're ready to start the walk. There is a junction of three roads beside a telephone box, and you'll find a signpost there.

1. Leave Clonbur by following the R345 road signposted for Corr na Mona. You pass a couple of shops, pubs and restaurants if you need any food or drink for your lunch pack. The road rises from the village and you'll see Mount Gable's bulky shape off to the right. A narrow road on the right is signposted for Carrowkeel and there is also a large sign at this junction advertising Burke's Pub back in Clonbur **(10mins)**.

2. Follow the narrow road uphill in the direction of Mount Gable, passing a few houses and farms. You'll see a waymark post with an arrow directing you to the right. The road dips down and up, then you reach another minor road junction where there is a signpost for Ballard. A waymark post points to the right, which would lead you to Lough Coolin, but you should turn left for Ballard **(35mins)**.

3. As the narrow road rises across the slopes of Mount Gable, there are views southwards across the island-studded Lough Corrib. There are a few houses along the way, and you should look out for a ladder stile beside a gate on the right. This is the key to the ascent of Mount Gable **(50mins)**.

4. Follow a grassy ribbon of a track uphill, watching carefully for its course whenever beds of rushes obscure the line. There are a couple of zig-zag sections, and some parts of the old track are buttressed with stonework. It was obviously an important track in its time as there are so many signs of engineering, but maps generally only show the lower part of it. The track finally reaches the high crest of Mount Gable, so that you can see both Lough Corrib and Lough Mask **(1hr 20mins)**.

    Note the short, low lengths of drystone walling dotted around the slopes of Mount Gable. These little walls are common in the area and were once used to shelter stacks of turf cut from the blanket bog on the mountain. The turf stacks were usually tied down with nets to stop them being blown away by gales in such exposed locations.

5. By swinging left and walking along the crest of Mount Gable, you pass a cairn on a hummock. In mist you could easily convince yourself that this was the summit, but in fact you need to keep walking along the boggy, hummocky crest, passing a pool of water and aiming for a concrete trig point at 416m (1,370ft) on the true summit **(1hr 40mins)**.

    There is a fine view from the summit, taking in Lough Corrib to the south, along with the long moorland rise of Cruach Mordain. Beyond the head of Lough Corrib are the Maum Turk Mountains, with peeps beyond to more distant mountains in Connemara. The vast, bleak plateau of Maumtrasna gives way to the broad expanse of Lough Mask.

If you wish to have lunch on the summit, then the time allowance given for the walk includes an hour on the summit. In the event of foul weather, you'd be better continuing with the walk and break for lunch in a more sheltered spot beside Lough Coolin.

6. Leave the summit trig point and head for a nearby cairn where you can overlook Lough Coolin. Pick a way downhill on the steep and rugged slope. Aim for the shore of Lough Coolin, but stay on the grassy slopes and avoid any rock outcrops on the way down. A track on the lower slopes leads to the shore of Lough Coolin. Head for a huddle of ruined cottages off to the left (**3hrs**).

    Looking round the steep slopes above Lough Coolin, in the right kind of light, you can spot the parallel lines of old potato ridges, some of them on very steep and high ground. The old ridges are mute testimony to the huge population Ireland boasted up to the Great Famine. The ruined cottages were abandoned at the same time.

7. There is a rugged path around the shore of Lough Coolin. At first it is enclosed by tumbled drystone walls, then it continues through bracken and heather. Towards the foot of the lake the old track is a clear and obvious line, but in places it has been overwhelmed by bog and is covered in squelchy sphagnum moss. You can either walk alongside the outflowing river, or cross two stony causeways at the foot of the lake, then cross back over the river to continue (**3hrs 15mins**).

8. A good track continues downstream, drifting away from the river beside a patchy conifer plantation. Beyond a gate, a narrow tarmac road runs downhill, passing a few houses and a roadside well. The road is very quiet and is actually grass-grown in places. When you reach a junction at the bottom, a waymark post points left, but you should turn right instead (**4hrs**).

9. At the next junction, turn left to reach a wider road, then turn right. This road carries a bit more traffic and leads past a Gaelic Football ground and cemetery, then is flanked by high stone walls as it reaches Clonbur. There are a handful of paces offering food and drink around the village (**5hrs**).

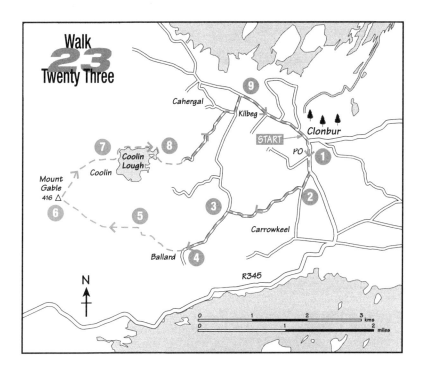

Other walks in the area

A copy of the Joyce Country Map Guide can be obtained locally, offering details of short, easy walks around the area. There are also interesting walks around the village of Cong, wandering through woods, beside rivers, visiting caves and other features of interest.

Places of interest

Ashford Castle is the most exclusive place to stay in the area, and a fine building too. Cong Abbey is in ruins, and there are many features of archaeological interest in the area. The film 'The Quiet Man' was shot in the area and still attracts devotees to the area.

Walk 24:
Inishmore & Dun Aengus
A cliffhanger adventure

The Aran Islands are three low-lying limestone rafts in the Atlantic Ocean. The most popular island is Inishmore, which is not to say the other two are any less scenic or interesting, but Inishmore is the one most people head for. You can complete a fine walk around the middle of the island, starting from the pier at Kilronan. You can walk an easy stretch of the Aran Islands Way along roads and tracks to Kilmurvey, then visit the cliff-edge fort of Dun Aengus. The cliffs are remarkable, overhanging for the most part, and repay careful exploration. After an exciting traverse along the cliffs, you can follow quiet tracks and roads back to Kilronan.

Grade: Moderate

Distance: 20km (12½ miles)

Time: 7 hours (including an hour for lunch)

Start & Finish: The pier at Kilronan 885089

Maps: Ordnance Survey of Ireland Discovery 51 and Ordnance Survey of Ireland 1:25,000 Aran Islands Map

How to get there

By car: Cars cannot be taken to Inishmore. To reach the ferryport at Rosaveal, follow the R336 road west of Galway city. Once you are through Inverin look out for one of two turnings on the left signposted for Rosaveal.

By bus: Bus Éireann table number 424 runs from Galway city, but doesn't quite reach Rosaveal as it stays on the R336 road. However, there are buses offering a direct link from the Tourist Information Office in Galway city to the ferryport at Rosaveal. Once you are on Inishmore, almost any minibus you see is actually a bus service ready to take you wherever you want to go on the island.

By ferry: Island Ferries run daily services all year round between Rosaveal and Kilronan. There are other ferries from other places, such as Galway city and Doolin, but they only operate seasonally. Contact Island Ferries on 091-561767.

By air: Aer Arann operate daily flights to Inishmore from a small airport at Inverin on the R336 road west of Galway city. If you take a short flight to the island then you should use one of the minibus services to get from the airport to Kilronan. Contact Aer Arann on 091-593034.

Necessities: Boots as the cliffs are very rocky; **walking shoes** will be fine for the roads and tracks; **waterproofs** as some parts of the walk are exposed in rain; **food and drink** can be purchased at Kilmurvey if the restaurant is open; **money** for the visitor centre; **ferry timetables** so you don't miss the boat.

Notes: The walk around the middle of Inishmore makes use of a couple of stretches of the waymarked Aran Islands Way. The walk along the cliffs is exceptionally rocky and you should beware of unseen overhangs, fractures and loose rock. Special care should be exercised near the cliff edges if there are strong winds.

Introduction

Inishmore can appear very busy when you're around places like Kilronan and Dun Aengus in the summer months, but there are always places you can reach that aren't too crowded, and if you visit out of season you could have the place to yourself. Inishmore became very popular in the 1930s following the shooting of the film 'Man of Aran', but if you look back over several centuries, it looks as though it has always been a popular place. It was a notable centre of learning in Dark Age Europe, attracting scholars from as far away as Rome.

Archaeological remains on the island are on a grand scale. The cliff-fort of Dun Aengus is visited on this walk, but there are a handful of other huge stone forts on the island, either circular ones in high places, or semi-circular ones on cliff edges. Dun Aengus is particularly impressive and you can have a look at a visitor centre dedicated to it at Kilmurvey. There are several ruined churches scattered across the island, and again the walk passes close to a couple of good examples; Teampall Chiaráin, Teampall Asurnaí, Teampall Mac Duach and Teampall Na Naomh. There are also smaller Christian monuments such as cross slabs.

Wildlife is also prominent on the walk. In early summer the limestone grasslands and pavements support of wealth of flowers, and the tiny fields are resplendent with tall grasses and buttercups. Water is scarce in the fields, so rainwater has to be collected in specially built troughs, but there are small pools along the way that are often frequented by wildfowl. A shingle beach at Portcowrugh often has seals hauled up on it and the shores generally feature a variety of birds.

The cliffs really are magnificent and you might want to explore them in more detail. You'll notice a tremendous overhang all the way round An Sunda Caoch; the Blind Sound. You'll also see the rectangular trough of Poll na bPéist, or the Worm Hole, with water slopping around from side to side. It looks man-made, but is in fact a natural phenomenon, fed by the sea being forced through bedding planes in the limestone bedrock. If you feel drawn to make a closer inspection, by doubling back along the rocky platform at the foot of the cliffs, be very wary of the sea, as incoming tides and big waves can cut you off.

You might choose to complete this walk without carrying any food or drink, relying instead on the fare at the restaurant at Kilmurvey. If you do this, you should check that it will be open before you leave Kilronan. The Tourist Information Office near the quay should be able to advise. If you have any time to spare at the end of the walk, or more likely, if you are staying overnight on the island, then you could go to the Heritage Centre in Kilronan and watch the classic 'Man of Aran' film.

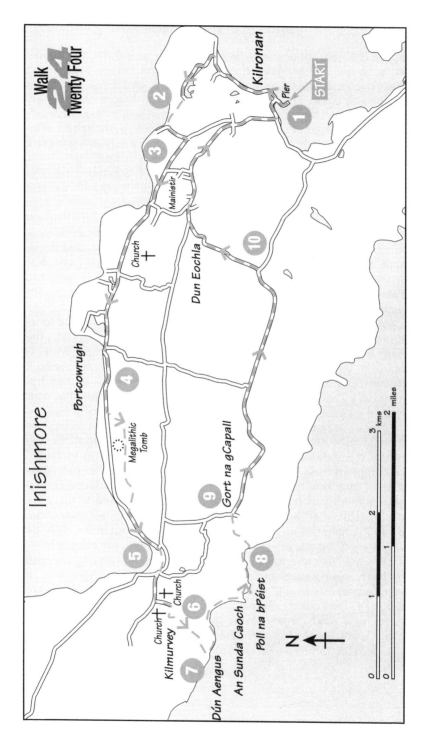

The Walk

When you step onto the pier at Kilronan, make sure you know the times of the return ferries. There are bars and restaurants readily to hand if you want food or drink before starting walking. Minibuses are ready to take you to any part of the island if you wish.

1. When you leave the pier, turn right and walk along a narrow, patchy road around the coast, away from the bustle at Kilronan. The road runs round a rocky point and alongside a shingle shore, and you should keep an eye on the line of telegraph poles alongside. When the poles turn left along another narrow road, you should turn left too, passing a couple of houses and continuing along a track enclosed by drystone walls. You walk beside a shallow pool of water and the track swings around its head **(30mins)**.

2. Turn right at a junction of tracks where you see a yellow 'walking man' painted on a wall. Follow the track to a small sandy beach at Mooltia. Cross the beach and come ashore, turning left to follow another track gently uphill and inland. Turn right along a minor road **(45mins)**.

   You'll notice plenty of small fields surrounded by drystone walls. You'll also see stone water troughs with a tilted ramp for collecting rainfall. Gates are beginning to appear in the fields, but you'll see some fields that apparently don't have gates in or out of them. If you look more carefully, you'll notice at least one section of rough walling, and that's the part the farmer knocks down and rebuilds when he wants to get in and out of his field.

3. Follow the minor road past the Aran Campsite. A grassy rise to the right of the road is crowned with an old cross slab. Further along the road, both signposted on the left, are the ruined churches of Teampall Chiaráin and Teampall Asurnaí, if you want to make slight detours to visit them. Even further along the road is a small lagoon separated from the sea by a shingle bank at Portcowrugh **(1hr 30mins)**.

   You can usually spot wildfowl on the lagoon, and swans often frequent the water. There may be seals on the seaward side, either in the water or hauled out on the shingle.

4. The road rises past a ruined building and runs gently downhill. Watch for a track on the left, bounded by tall, ivy-covered walls, marked with a yellow 'walking man'. Walk gently uphill along the track, watching carefully for a gap in the wall on the right, also marked in yellow. Follow a narrow path along a lovely limestone terrace, which is covered in colourful flowers in early summer. The path leads onto a walled track that runs back down to the road, where you turn left to continue to Portmurvey **(2hrs 15mins)**.

The rectangular stone trough of Poll na bPéist on Inishmore

5. Walk along the top of the sea wall around the sandy bay, then follow a road uphill and inland, which is signposted for Dun Aengus. The road passes an old graveyard, then you turn right at a huddle of craft shops. Kilmurvey House offers accommodation alongside, and you can make short detours at this point to look at the ancient ruined churches of Teampall Mac Duach and Teampall Na Naomh. At the end of the road you reach An Sunda Caoch Restaurant and the Dun Aengus Visitor Centre **(2hrs 30mins)**.

If you want to enquire into the history of Dun Aengus, then you can pop into the visitor centre and take on board some information about the site. While you're within easy reach of An Sunda Caoch Restaurant, you might prefer to break at this point for lunch. The time allowance for the walk assumes you'll spend an hour at this point, though you might want to add a bit extra for time spent at the visitor centre.

6. Follow a broad gravel path uphill from the visitor centre to Dun Aengus **(3hrs 45mins)**.

Spend a while exploring the site, taking in its triple ramparts and fearsome spiky 'chevaux de frise' defences on the western side. As you pass through the final portal, you reach a level grassy area, where your attention seems to be directed to a natural rocky platform on the very edge of the cliff. Scholars have argued about whether the site was built for defence, or served some ritual purpose.

The 'chevaux de frise' and triple ramparts suggest defence, but the raised rock platform and splendid amphitheate inside suggest a ritual use. Perhaps it was both. It is certainly spectacular and very popular with visitors.

7. Walk downhill from Dun Aengus, around the curved and severely undercut cliffs of An Sunda Caoch. The sea always seems to be boiling here, exploding against the base of the cliffs. Indeed, one stormy night the waves came in so furiously that they broke over the lip of the cliff and water swilled across the island to Portmurvey! You walk on limestone terraces and boulder-strewn pavements. After turning round a rocky point you can overlook the rectangular hole of Poll na bPéist and marvel that such a regular feature could have been formed entirely by natural forces **(4hrs 30mins)**.

8. Continue along the cliff line and head gradually downhill to reach a lower part of the rocky coastline.

   If you wanted to double back along the base of the cliffs, with extreme care, then you could visit Poll na bPéist. Things you need to watch include the sea, which is unpredictable; the undercut cliffs, which are bound to collapse one day; and the rock platform, which is treacherously slippery for much of its length. You have been warned, and you should be reminded to add an extra half-hour for the diversion.

   More cautious walkers will be happy to head inland. You need to look very carefully in this rocky terrain to spot a gravel track on the limestone pavement, then switch to a walled track that leads to the little settlement of Gort na gCapall **(5hrs)**.

9. When you join a narrow tarmac road in Gort na gCapall, turn right to follow it away from the houses, rising gradually uphill through the centre of Inishmore. The tarmac gives way to a gravelly, grassy surface and the broad track is flanked by stone walls as it passes dozens of tiny fields. At times there are no settlements in sight, and you keep walking down into a dip, then uphill and swing to the left. There is a pronounced right bend on the way downhill **(6hrs)**.

10. Turn left at a point where tracks intersect. Follow a track that rises gently, then descends a short way to join the main road through the island at Mainistir. Turn right and follow the road down past the Mainistir Hostel on the way back into the village of Kilronan. If you're thinking of catching a ferry, then you may need to hurry down to the pier. If you're staying longer on the island, maybe for a couple of days, then you can get to know all the bars and restaurants in turn **(7hrs)**.

Other walks in the area

The cliff coast of Inishmore offers a truly amazing walk, but it is rough and rocky from end to end. The waymarked Aran Islands Ways offer walks on all three islands, and you can obtain the Aran Islands Ways Map Guide for details. There is enough walking to keep you on the islands for a week or more.

Places of interest

There is an interesting Heritage Centre at Kilronan, where you can watch the 'Man of Aran' film. Inishmore is liberally scattered with archaeological remains, and there are minibus tours available to all the main sites.

Walk 25:
The Castlebar International
Four-Day Walks
Walk with the world

Since being founded in 1967, the Castlebar International Four-Day Walks has grown to become Ireland's premier walking event. It takes place over the first weekend in July each year and is attended by around 1,500 walkers from over 20 different countries. They come in ones and twos, or as members of walking clubs, or military marching teams wearing uniforms. They descend on Castlebar to enjoy four days of walks, and five nights of hectic entertainment! Everyone's welcome; it is a non-competitive event with no winners and no losers, and there's nothing else quite like it in Ireland.

Grade: Moderate

Distances: Around 30km (18 miles)

Time: Around 8 hours

Start & Finish: The Welcome Inn at Castlebar 146908

Map: Ordnance Survey of Ireland Discovery 31

How to get there

By car: Castlebar is on the main N5 road between Sligo and Westport. Anyone travelling from Dublin and Athlone would arrive via the N60 road. Travelling from Galway, you could use the N84 road, or the scenic N59 road through Connemara.

By bus: Bus Éireann table number 21 links Castlebar with Dublin and Westport. Table number 51 links with Ballina, Galway and Cork. Table number 66 links with Achill Island and Sligo. Table number 69 links with Sligo and Belfast.

By train: Castlebar has an Iarnród Éireann station on the line from Dublin to Westport.

By air: Walkers can arrive for the walks via Knock Airport, and if they give due notice to the organisers, they can be collected by arrangement and brought in to Castlebar.

Necessities: Boots as parts of the walks can be boggy; **walking shoes** are recommended for roads and tracks; **waterproofs** as there's little shelter from the rain; **food** for the day as drinks are provided at regular refreshments stops.

Notes: The Castlebar International Four-Day Walks take place over the first weekend in July. The cross-country rambles are guided and it is important to follow the instructions of the leaders and not to deviate from the routes. There is full emergency radio cover and medical assistance. There is an entry fee for the walks which covers all services associated with the walks, as well as the evening entertainment. For full details contact the organisers on 094-24102.

Introduction

The Castlebar International Four-Day Walks started small in 1967, with only a handful of local walkers joined by a few Dutch friends. Slow and steady growth has brought the walks an attendance of 1,500 walkers, with over 20 countries regularly represented. Walkers from all over Ireland join local walkers, and there is a significant Dutch presence. There are walkers from almost every European country, as well as Japanese, Americans, Australians and New Zealanders. The Castlebar walks are allied to the International Marching League (IML) and the Internationaler Volkssportverband (IVV); and these world-wide connections ensure that they'll grow from strength to strength.

The format for the walks is well established. Walkers arrive on the Wednesday evening and get settled into pre-booked accommodation. You take a big chance turning up in Castlebar without booking ahead, as every single bed is likely to be occupied! On the Wednesday evening there is a briefing session, and any walkers who haven't already registered will find it is best to do so before the walks actually commence. With great pomp and circumstance, there is a parade around the town in the evening led by a military band, and everyone's awake to the fact that the walks are on!

The format for the walks is as follows. There are a series of colour-coded, self-guided road-walks, set at various distances. These head off into all parts of the countryside around Castlebar. Youngsters and late starters can walk as little as 10km (6 miles). There are longer 20km and 40km (12 and 25 mile) walks in wider loops. The longer walks earn greater credits under the IVV system, where points are earned for distance covered and events attended. The IML has its own system of awards for events attended, and the Castlebar walks themselves have a system of bronze, silver and gold medals.

The most popular walks are undoubtedly the cross-country rambles. These measure around 30km (18 miles) and head into the countryside north of Castlebar. They start at 9am each day and you're required to finish by 5pm. There are low, boggy hills, small forests, farmland and quiet country roads. In fine weather the views can be quite extensive, but in mist and rain there's little to see. The cross-country rambles are guided for the most part, but towards the end the walkers are turned loose to follow quiet roads back to town at their own pace.

Always, the sheer spectacle of so many walkers trailing over the hills and along the roads and tracks is a sight to behold. Some of them carry flags, wear promotional gear, or are covered in cloth badges collected at other walking events around the world. You'll be surrounded by people speaking a dozen languages, and the chance to make contact with walkers from all over the world is part of the attraction of the walks.

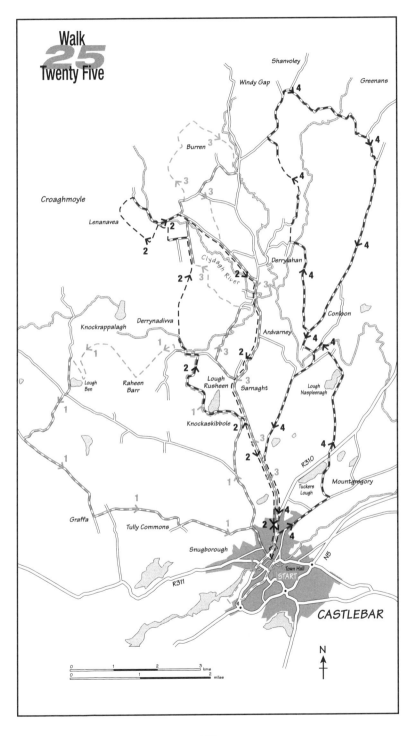

Walk
25
Twenty Five

Shanvoley
Windy Gap
Greenans
4
4
Burren **3**
3
4
Croaghmoyle
3
4
Lenanavea
2
2
Clydagh River
Derrylahan
2
2
3
3
4
Conloon
Derrynadivva
Ardvarney
4
Knockrappalagh
1
3
2
4
2
Lough
Ben
Raheen
Barr
1
2
Lough
Rusheen
Sarnaght
Lough
Naspleenagh
1
1
Knockaskibbole **2**
4
3
4
1
2
R310
3
1
Tuckers
Lough
Mountgregory
Graffa
Tully Commons
1
2
4
Snugborough
4
Town Hall
N5
START
R311
CASTLEBAR
N

0 1 2 3 kms
0 1 2 miles

147

The Walks

Remember that you should pre-register for the walks and pre-book your accommodation, then all you have to do is turn up for the walks and enjoy the spectacle as you walk with the world at Castlebar.

Walkers on the Red Hopkins walk with Burren Mountain beyond

Day 1 – Thursday – Raheen Barr

The first of the four-day walks is over Raheen Barr. The walkers leave Castlebar by way of Castlebar Lough, then walk along quiet country roads. After a drinks stop they switch to a bog road and walk round the little Lough Rusheen, where their figures reflect in the water. After that they're led up the broad and boggy slopes of Raheen Barr for their first panoramic views of the surrounding countryside. The sight of so many walkers snaking up the slopes is amazing, with their flags flying in the breeze. There is a break on top of the hill, which is only 243 m (799 ft), but the views seem to stretch forever across the lowlands, and the conical peak of Croagh Patrick is also prominent.

Moving down the hill, the walkers are led in a broad arc around the neighbouring hill of Knockrappalaghaun to reach a point overlooking little Lough Ben. Picking their way round the steep slopes above the lough, they walk down to a minor road for a lunch break. Quiet roads are linked as the walkers head back to Castlebar via Graffa, Tully Commons and Snugborough.

Day 2 – Friday – Red Hopkins

On the second day's walk everyone leaves town and another series of quiet roads and tracks are linked to approach the hills. Lough Rusheen is passed again, followed by a drinks stop. There is a stretch over a soft bog, and special stiles are erected over fences along the way. After another drinks stop, the walkers are led onto a broad and boggy rise called Lenanavea, which rises to 324m (1,063ft). Whirling windmills have been planted here, generating electricity. After a break on top, and another chance to observe sweeping views, the walkers are led round in a loop and down into a valley, returning to the last drink stop, only this time to take a lunch break.

The name Red Hopkins, incidentally, was the name of a man who lived in a remote house in the valley. After lunch the walkers follow a road parallel to the Clydagh River and make their own way back to Castlebar via Sarnaght. There are little rises on the road where you can look back and look ahead, and all you see are hundreds of walkers all heading back to town.

Day 3 – Saturday – Burren Mountain

This is the most popular and scenic of the cross-country rambles. While the international walkers have been in Castlebar right from the start, along with most of the local walkers, there is a sudden increase in numbers as walkers from all other parts of Ireland turn up just for the weekend. The days walk starts by linking minor roads on the way out of town, through Sarnaght, switching to bog roads and forest tracks. A lunch break is taken near the foot of Burren Mountain. Climbing up the steep and rugged slopes of Burren Mountain, the walkers reach a gap at 320m (1,050ft). There is a splendid view through the gap to the domed mountain of Nephin, with Lough Conn filling the lowland landscape. After moving across the rough and heathery slopes, the walkers cascade downhill and pick their way downstream alongside the Clydagh River to reach an old bridge for a drinks stop.

After walking through a forest and across an open bog, the walkers are let loose to make their way back to town along the roads. They cross the Clydagh River and walk through Sarnaght to return to Castlebar, and by this time they realise they are covering roads they already know from previous days.

Day 4 – Sunday – The Sunday Ramble

The Sunday Ramble is essentially a low-level walk, but it is a little longer than the rest of the walks in the series. Minor roads and tracks are used to leave Castlebar, passing Tucker's Lough and Lough Naspleenagh. A point is reached where steeping stones can be used to cross the Clydagh River, though if there has been any rain and the river is running high, the walk detours round by road. There is a drinks stop at Conloon. As the route heads through Derrylahan and Cummauns, there are views of Burren Mountain across the valley, then there is a lunch break at Shanvoley. At this point, there is usually an informal presentation made to any walkers who are gaining major awards later in the evening.

The walkers are let loose one last time to follow a lengthy series of roads back to Castlebar. There is a winding hill road to negotiate first around Tawnykinaff, then a more direct line leads back past Conloon, across the Clydagh River and back to Castlebar. There is a chance for congratulations before the walkers get cleaned up for the grand finale.

The last part of the Castlebar International Four-Day Walks is the formal presentation of awards. There are silver and gold Castlebar medals, as well as IML awards, which include European Walker, International Walker and International Master Walker. After the formalities and closing ceremony, the Blister Ball commences, with music and dancing for those who are still able to stand on their own two feet and dance the night away!

Other walks in the area

Castlebar is within easy reach of Westport, for links with the Western Way and Croagh Patrick; Foxford and Bellavary, for links with the Foxford Way; Kiltimagh, which has a selection of easy walks; and Ballintubber Abbey, which has walks and a pilgrimage trail.

Places of interest

When the Castlebar walks are in full swing, no-one has any time for any other places of interest!

In the same series:

Each book costs £9.95 and contains a superb range of walks.

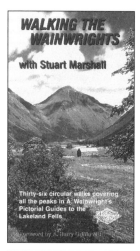

Holiday Walks in the UK too – a small selection from our BIG catalogue!

WALKING THE WAINWRIGHTS: A Field Guide

Stuart Marshall

This ground-breaking book is a scheme of walks linking all of the 214 peaks in the late Alfred Wainwright's seven-volume *Pictorial Guide to The Lakeland Fells*. After an introduction to the Lake District, the route descriptions are clearly presented with the two-colour sketch maps facing the descriptive text – so that the book can be carried flat in a standard map case. The walks average 12 miles in length but the more demanding ones are presented both as one-day and two-day excursions. £7.95

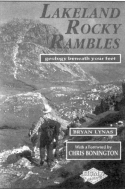

LAKELAND ROCKY RAMBLES: Geology beneath your feet

Bryan Lynas;
Foreword by Chris Bonington

This is the companion book to Snowdonia Rocky Rambles: the perfect way to learn about why things look the way they do. "Refreshing ... Ambitious ... Informative ... Inspiring" NEW SCIENTIST. £9.95

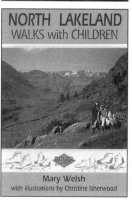

NORTH LAKELAND WALKS WITH CHILDREN

Mary Welsh;
illustrations by Christine Isherwood

"It has been great fun speaking to children I have met on the walks and listening to what they have to say" says Mary Welsh. Her refreshing, enthusiastic attitude is reflected in her book, written specifically with the needs, entertainment and safety of children in mind. Perfect for parents of reluctant walkers. £6.95

See earlier for ordering information

BEST TEA SHOP WALKS IN NOTTINGHAMSHIRE

Paul & Sandra Biggs

"... the collection of Sigma's tea shop walk books already includes ones on the Peak District and Staffordshire...... Here they range through Robin Hood country; see various stately parklands in the Dukeries... and at Wellow, the 62ft high maypole on the village green." DERBY EVENING TELEGRAPH With walks ranging from 2-9 miles, detailed walking instructions, clear maps and attractive photographs, each route contains details of a charming tea shop where you can enjoy a delicious home-made cream tea. £6.95

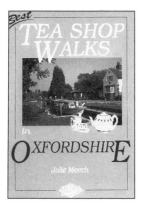

BEST TEA SHOP WALKS IN OXFORDSHIRE

Julie Meech

The Cotswolds, the Chilterns, the Thames Valley and even a small share of the Wessex Downs – all these are to be found in Oxfordshire, yet the county's great potential for walkers is often not fully appreciated. The 25 walks in this new guide explore all the different facets of this varied county, and all include the additional pleasure of a stop for afternoon tea. Every walk is easily accessible by public transport, and many are within easy reach of London – the ideal excuse to escape from the city for a few hours! £6.95

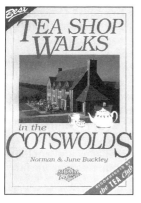

TEA SHOP WALKS IN THE COTSWOLDS

Norman & June Buckley

No other area in Britain has as many tea shops as the Cotswolds. This new book of 26 walks takes the reader the length and breadth of the area, visiting the popular towns and tiny villages. The walks average 5-6 miles and each features a tea shop that welcomes walkers.   £6.95

See earlier for ordering information

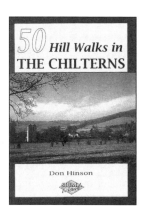

50 HILL WALKS IN THE CHILTERNS

Don Hinson

Routes specially chosen to give comprehensive coverage of scenic areas, clear maps and route descriptions, interesting details for each walk, and a checklist of items that you might require – all you could possibly desire for the perfect day out in the unspoilt landscape of the rolling Chiltern hills. £6.95

A YEAR OF WALKS: Kent

Roy Woodcock

Keep in step with nature as you explore Kent throughout the seasons. Twelve superb routes, one for each month of the year, plus several with short-cut options to allow them to be completed in half a day. None of the routes is strenuous – all ideal for family excursions, covering a wide range of scenic locations across the county and visiting coastlines from the chalk cliff of the south to reclaimed marshes in the north. Informed commentary highlights features of interest – historical, geographical or man-made. £6.95

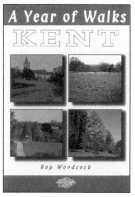

DAY WALKS ON THE SOUTH DOWNS

John Allen

The only book of one-day circular walks currently available for the South Downs. The guide's 31 detailed walk plans come complete with sketch maps and provide a thorough exploration of the Downs between Beacon Hill in Hampshire and Beachy Head. 28 of the walks are full-day, while three shorter routes explore out-of-the way corners. All have been designed to take in both countryside and places of interest nearby – so there's plenty of opportunity to visit the area's unspoilt villages and ancient churches. A detailed commentary gives full background information on the area – as well as those essential practical bits: opening times, parking etc. £7.95

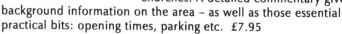

See earlier for ordering information